ar

at

After Bloody Sunday

JL: To Niall
TH: To Juliet

After Bloody Sunday
Ethics, Representation, Justice

TOM HERRON

and

JOHN LYNCH

First published in November 2007 by
Cork University Press
Youngline Industrial Estate
Pouladuff Road, Togher
Cork, Ireland

British Library Cataloguing in Publication Data.
A CIP catalogue record for this book is available from the British Library

ISBN–13: 978-1-85918-425-7

The authors have asserted their moral rights in this work.

Typeset by Tower Books, Ballincollig, Co. Cork
Printed by ColourBooks Ltd, Baldoyle, Co. Dublin

www.corkuniversitypress.com

Contents

Illustrations

Acknowledgements

We would like to thank Adrian Kerr and John Kelly of the Museum of Free Derry/Bloody Sunday Trust for their time and insights when we were gathering material for the book. We would like to thank Tom Dunne, who helped initiate this project at Cork University Press, and Sophie Watson, who saw it through to completion. Thanks are also due to Gloria Greenwood and Winifred Power. Thanks to the Dublin Gallery of Photography and the organisers of the 'Representing the Troubles' conference at the Royal Irish Academy (April 2003) for inviting us to present our initial thoughts on some of the material at the very early stages of the project. Thanks also to Malachy McDaid, of the Council for the Curriculum, Examinations and Assessment (Belfast), who designed the virtual reality system used at the new Bloody Sunday Inquiry and who took the time to explain to us its development and use. Finally, thanks to Lance Pettitt.

John Lynch would like to thank Ross Abbinnett, Simon O'Sullivan, Pete Webb, Mathew Caygill, Mairtin Mac An Ghaill and John Holmwood for advice and discussion of many of the ideas contained in the book, Jill Summers for her encouragement and Joan and Edward Lynch for their love and support. Very special thanks to Emilia, who is a constant source of inspiration and enthusiastic argument.

Tom Herron would like to thank Julieann Campbell of *The Derry Journal*; Dave Duggan of Sole Productions, Derry; Angela Hegarty of the School of Law, University of Ulster; Jim Collins of the Bloody Sunday Weekend Committee/Bluebell Arts, Derry; Michael Herron for the first edition of *Butcher's Dozen*, Will Kelly of the Bogside Artists, Jim McCole for the long-term 'loan' of *Sometime in New York City*; and Nick Cox. Particular thanks go to Juliet for her love and support.

A version of Chapter One appeared in the *Journal of Cultural Research*, and parts of Chapter Two in *Visual Culture in Britain*. We thank both editors for permission to reproduce this material.

Tom Herron and John Lynch,
November 2007

Those killed and injured on Bloody Sunday

THOSE KILLED ON BLOODY SUNDAY

Patrick ('Paddy') Doherty (31)
Gerald Donaghy (17)
John ('Jackie') Duddy (17)
Hugh Gilmore (17)
Michael Kelly (17)
Michael McDaid (20)
Kevin McElhinney (17)
Bernard ('Barney') McGuigan (41)
Gerald McKinney (35)
William ('Willie') McKinney (26)
William Nash (19)
James ('Jim') Wray (22)
John Young (17)
John Johnston (59) (died later of his injuries)

THOSE INJURED ON BLOODY SUNDAY

Michael Bradley (22)
Michael Bridge (25)
Alana Burke (18)
Patrick Campbell (53)
Margaret ('Peggy') Deery (37)
Damien Donaghy (15)
Joseph ('Joe') Friel (20)
Daniel Gillespie (31)
Joseph Mahon (16)
Patrick McDaid (24)
Daniel McGowan (37)
Alexander ('Alex') Nash (52)
Patrick ('Paddy') O'Donnell (41)
Michael Quinn (17)

Introduction

'Bloody Sunday' in the title of this book refers to the afternoon of Sunday 30 January 1972, when thirteen men and boys participating in a civil rights march in Derry, Northern Ireland, were shot dead by soldiers of the British Army. A further fifteen people were seriously injured, one of whom died several months later of injuries received on the day. The British Army officer in charge of the operation claimed that his men had opened fire only after having come under attack from armed republicans, a view that was rapidly endorsed by British and Northern Irish government ministers. Almost every eyewitness to the events – protesters, journalists, photographers, bystanders, residents – said that the army had fired indiscriminately and without provocation into crowds of unarmed civilians, many of them fleeing from the soldiers' advance into the no-go Bogside area of Derry. A hastily arranged judicial inquiry set up by the British government found largely in favour of the army. The inquiry's chairman, Lord Chief Justice Widgery, concluded that, although some of the soldiers' behaviour had at times 'bordered on the reckless',[1] their actions, in the face of a sustained attack by IRA gunmen and hooligan nail-bombers, were safely within the British Army's rules of engagement. Whilst none of the dead were proven to have been handling firearms or nail-bombs, Lord Widgery concluded that 'there is a strong suspicion that some . . . had been firing weapons or handling bombs'.[2] One of the dead, according to Widgery, had been found with nail-bombs on him when his body was examined by an army medical officer. No soldiers were injured during the operation.

For the Catholic/nationalist community of Derry[3] what had taken place on the streets of their city was nothing short of a massacre of unarmed civilians by soldiers with a reputation for brutality.[4] This sense of grievance was compounded by Lord Widgery's report, in which, according to Fr Edward Daly (an eyewitness to some of the killings), 'the guilty were found to be innocent. The innocent were found to be guilty.'[5] Seen by many people as either an overly hasty and flawed interpretation of the facts set out before the tribunal, or as a whitewash of

1

state-engendered atrocity, the Widgery Report accelerated the sense of alienation felt by the Catholic/nationalist community from the state processes of law and order, and in turn contributed to an exponential increase in membership of the IRA, who now took on the mantle of guardians of that community. With a pusillanimous Irish government, and a Northern police militia that had, over the years, shown little hesitation in intimidating Catholics and attacking nationalist neighbourhoods, and a legal system that exonerated state murder, who else would now defend the embattled northern community from the forces of the British/Northern Irish state and their legal apparatuses? As a statement by the Derry-based Bloody Sunday Initiative puts it, Bloody Sunday was:

> a microcosm, a symbol of what Britain does in Ireland. The British state and its agencies still kill people, deliberately, as a matter of policy without any compunction, often with no regret. It kills as a first step not as a last resort. It systematically manipulates the judicial processes of the courts or inquests in order that the law becomes an instrument to exonerate the state for its actions . . . It establishes inquiries to conceal what has happened and to exonerate those responsible. It censors and distorts the view of those who disagree with it.[6]

Bloody Sunday and its official inscription in the Widgery Report were pivotal moments in the development of the Northern Ireland 'Troubles' from a relatively low-intensity conflict to a situation in which a guerrilla campaign and counter-terrorism war contributed towards the breakdown of civil society (it is, of course, questionable how a society founded on sectarian lines can ever, actually, be 'civil'). Throughout the early years of the conflict (1968–1972) an active, if disparate, civil rights movement garnered support from those who retained a faith in peacefully reforming – through the diverse tactics of protest and civil disobedience – an institutionally discriminatory state. And although it is true to say that the civil rights movement persisted after Bloody Sunday, it is equally true to say that the events in the Bogside on 30 January 1972 revealed the limits of peaceful protest in the face of a state that had little interest in reforming itself, and that had no hesitation in deploying brutal, and now lethal, force to quell dissident voices. In the three years prior to Bloody Sunday 210 people had been killed in the conflict; in the eleven months after Bloody Sunday some 445 people lost their lives. In every sense, Bloody Sunday can be seen as a turning-point.

Our intention in this book is not to tell or retell the story of Bloody Sunday; the people of Derry are themselves quite capable of remembering, sharing and relating the many stories that make up the larger narrative of that day. (We would direct readers to a number of books that provide detailed accounts of the day and the devastating effects it had on the lives of so many people.) *After Bloody Sunday* investigates the ways in which the events in Derry on 30 January 1972 have been imagined, renegotiated and represented across a range of media and cultural processes – photography, film, theatre, poetry, murals, commemorative events, legal discourse, eyewitness testimony and pressure-group campaigns. Some of these products and processes have been produced by Derry people (the Bogside murals, the annual commemorative events and the establishment of the Museum of Free Derry are the most notable examples), whilst others have been produced by people from beyond the city (most of the films and documentaries fall into this category). In this book we are concerned primarily with the *dissemination* of Bloody Sunday as a particularly resonant and, indeed, iconic event. We are concerned with how Bloody Sunday is narrativised, and with how the many representations attempt to establish a particularly persuasive version of the events of that day. We are concerned with their claims and their mechanisms for producing 'authenticity' and, therefore, veridicity. We are interested in their assumptions that a particular medium – be it film, or literature, or photography – can, somehow, remember and then articulate the 'truth' of Bloody Sunday. This assertion of truth-value is a key component of almost every representation we consider. And it is hardly surprising that, in the face of a blatant perversion of the truth-finding function of the law, culture and art have filled the gap with versions of a popular, demotic history of Bloody Sunday, versions that (again with differences of emphasis) sustain an oppositional version of the events and contexts of Bloody Sunday to the official state version of the day.

The most ambitious attempt to meld these competing versions of Bloody Sunday has been the task of the new inquiry into the killings. Established in January 1998 by British Prime Minister Tony Blair and chaired by Lord Mark Saville of Newdigate, the Bloody Sunday Inquiry has been, without doubt, the most ambitious attempt to arrive at, and then 'to establish the truth about what happened on that day, so far as that can be achieved at 26 years' distance'.[7] Although this is possibly an illusory goal, the inquiry is regarded by most people who have had any dealings with it as the best chance of establishing a definitive account of Bloody Sunday. However, the fact that the anticipated publication of the final report has been pushed even further away – Saville and his two colleagues may not publish their report until 2008 – raises acute questions about the possibility of condensing into narrative (no matter how capacious or nuanced or complexly layered) the multiple and conflicting versions of the events of 30 January 1972. In a recent letter to representatives of the relatives of the killed and injured Lord Saville sets out the problems with which he and his team have had to deal:

> The hearings of the inquiry occupied 435 sitting days, during which the tribunal heard oral evidence on 367 days from 922 witnesses. In

the course of those hearings, approximately 14.5 million words were spoken. The tribunal received the evidence in writing of a further 1,563 witnesses who were not called to give oral evidence. The bundles of statements, documents and photographs comprise about 160 volumes. The tribunal also has before it 110 video tapes and 121 audio tapes. The written submissions of the interested parties and of counsel to the inquiry consist of more than 14,000 pages of detailed and complex argument. The tribunal has the formidable task of analysing this vast amount of evidence, assessing the reliability of the witnesses, determining so far as possible where the truth lies on hundreds of disputed issues, and giving a full and clear explanation of its reasoning and conclusions.[8]

In chairing the longest judicial inquiry in British history Lord Saville has a professional responsibility that artists, poets, filmmakers and muralists may of course share, but it is not a duty that they have to bear as an ethical imperative. Somehow or other, Saville must negotiate not only the sheer exorbitance of evidence, but also the abyss of meaning that opened up at the moment the soldiers trained their sights on the protesters. His version – which, let us be clear, must be the definitive version of both the events of the day and the circumstances that led to those events – has, on the one hand, to translate the silences, obfuscations, and lies of the British state into decipherable meaning, whilst, on the other, it has to ignore completely the shibboleths of victimhood and martyrology that for many years sustained the various campaigns for a fresh judicial inquiry into the killings. It is, to be sure, a formidable task, all the more formidable because it may be impossible.

One can, in fact, imagine a set of circumstances in which the dead, injured and traumatised of Bloody Sunday could have received, if not 'justice' then at the very least a recognition of the injustice perpetrated on the day, without the need for over three decades of campaigns by their supporters and without, over the same span of time, non-cooperation, intimidation and destruction of evidence by agencies of the British state. Because, on the face of it, Bloody Sunday was not an ungraspably complex event. Moreover, it was an event that was captured comprehensively in multiple media formats – television news, radio reports, photographically, journalistically. With the exception of the dreadful events in Glenfada Park, the shootings – which lasted no more than twenty minutes – were, as Lord Saville points out in his letter, well documented. In interviews and news conferences in the minutes and hours following the shootings, both sides (the British Army on the one side, and the protestors and eyewitnesses on the other) attempted to communicate to the large contingent of national and international media the truth of what had just happened. The official British version of events followed faithfully the initial (and entirely erroneous) comments of the Commander of British Land Forces in the North, Major-General Robert Ford who, whilst being questioned at an impromptu press conference by

John Bierman of the BBC, announced that the soldiers of the Parachute Regiment had responded in a restrained and responsible manner to murderous attacks upon them. Stressing that he was only present in Derry as an observer to the army operation, Major-General Ford stated to an incredulous Bierman that only three bullets had been fired by the army. This version of events, albeit with the dramatically increased body count factored in, was quickly taken up by most, but by no means all, of the British media. The Irish media, on the other hand, tended to highlight and support the views of those who presented a picture of disproportionate attack – eyewitness reports of the killings were given prominence in many Irish newspapers.

For a number of reasons it was the British version of events that predominated. It is important to understand the obvious but crucial point that the attack on the protesters took place on British territory. It was the British Army who had turned its high-velocity rifles on its own citizens; on citizens who, through their taxes, had paid for the upkeep of an army that had arrived on the streets of Derry and Belfast in August 1969 in order to protect the Catholic/nationalist community from attacks by their own police force, and now only seventeen months later was itself shooting unarmed British subjects protesting peacefully against the internment without trial of persons identified the previous year as having involvement with republicanism. That British soldiers had trained their guns on British subjects undoubtedly lent urgency to the Conservative government of Prime Minister Edward Heath to establish a tribunal of inquiry under the land's most senior law officer. Samuel Dash comments that 'there appears to be little or no parallel . . . to such an event involving British soldiers and British civilians,'[9] but one only has to think back to Dublin's Bloody Sunday (21 November 1920) and to Manchester's Peterloo Massacre (16 August 1819) to see direct parallels with the events in the Bogside. It is equally clear now that the official British Army and government version of events undoubtedly influenced the scope, the tenor and, it appears, the outcome of the tribunal of inquiry. The discovery in 1995 of a confidential Downing Street minute detailing a meeting on the evening of 1 February 1972 between British Prime Minister Heath, Lord Chancellor Hailsham and the Lord Chief Justice of England, Lord Widgery, revealed an apparently unembarrassed complicity between government and legal process. Just hours before announcing his intention to hold a tribunal of inquiry into the killings, Prime Minister Heath reminded Widgery that the morale of the army was at stake and that 'we were in Northern Ireland fighting not only a military war but a propaganda war'.[10]

The Widgery Report revealed how, given appropriate levels of support from a docile opposition and given insufficient investigative will from an obedient media, a powerful discursivity could operate and gain the upper hand, notwithstanding the fact that its interpretation of the evidence presented to a tribunal of inquiry was so grotesque. Even allowing for the entirely inadequate selection of witnesses,[11] Widgery was an affront not only to the victims it so eagerly sought to traduce, but also to the very basis of law and justice. In the face of a wealth of counter-evidence, national and international criticism, detailed legal critiques of its procedures and interpretations and the gradual erosion of the veridicity of its conclusions, the version of events that Widgery established remains, so far, the official truth of Bloody Sunday.

Bloody Sunday was not an isolated event. The events that led up to the day, the day itself, and the judicial whitewash must all be understood in the light of contemporary events that defined the period as one of intense and dangerous social turmoil. And whilst Bloody Sunday was a pivotal moment both in the development of the Northern Ireland Troubles and the concomitant dismantling of the Northern Ireland state, it would be invidious to privilege it over other atrocities that caused immense pain and long-term suffering to people of all parties, factions and sides of the conflict: as well as, of course, to those entirely non-aligned victims of violence. So, it is worthwhile asking the question, 'Why another book on Bloody Sunday?' Why are we not directing our energies to other 'harrowings of the heart',[12] such as the bombing of McGurk's bar in Belfast (December 1971), or the Bloody Friday bombing of Belfast (July 1972), or the Dublin and Monaghan bombs (May 1974), or the Birmingham pub bombings (November 1974), or the Remembrance Day bomb attack in Enniskillen (November 1987), or the Shankill Road bombing (October 1993), or the Omagh bombings (August 1998)? And there have been so many others on a smaller, if no less atrocious, scale; they are all there in David McKittrick's *Lost Lives* (1999), that terrible and poignant record of the many violent acts of the Northern Irish conflict. So, why Bloody Sunday?

'A number of things made Derry different', writes Eamonn McCann:

> This was a very British atrocity, and the biggest single killing by state forces in the course of the Troubles. The resultant affront was compounded by the fact that the British state at the highest level, in the person of the Lord Chief Justice, had then proclaimed that the killings were neither wrong nor illegal. In every other atrocity with which Bloody Sunday has regularly been compared or likened, the victims are acknowledged, more or less universally, as having been wrongly done to death and the perpetrators damned as wrongdoers. But the Bloody Sunday families were told, in effect, that while they might personally, reasonably, lament the loss of a loved one, they had no wider ground for grievance or legitimate expectation of the killers being punished. The state stood by its own. All the dead were thus diminished.[13]

It is this double injury – of a failure of justice compounded by the epistemological violence of Widgery's findings – that has prompted virtually all representation of Bloody Sunday. Anne Crilly and Angela Hegarty argue similarly:

> the failure of law and the appropriation of official discourse by the state led to the community affected by Bloody Sunday finding alternative ways to remember it and to tell its version of the truth. Having been denied what it regarded as a fair investigation into the events of Bloody Sunday and instead presented with an official version of events that contradicted hundreds of local eyewitnesses, the local community began to commemorate and document the events of Bloody Sunday in its own ways.[14]

The new Bloody Sunday Inquiry represents the first serious attempt by the British government to engage in the issues that have been taken up by artists, filmmakers, poets and campaigners over three decades. Much depends on the outcome of Mark Saville's long-awaited report, but in this book we are less concerned with a British government-sponsored narrative of Bloody Sunday and its context than with some of the processes at work within a range of differing and diverse examples of cultural negotiations produced since that day. In multiple and diverse ways, an after-image of this state atrocity has continued to be present as an event still unresolved, and as an event that demands attention, that requires response in the face of 'official' silence.

One of the key aspects of Bloody Sunday is the way in which it can be seen to exemplify a shift in strategy by the British government towards one of an increased militarisation of the province and the pacification of trouble spots such as the Bogside and the Creggan through surveillance, occupation and repression. Demands for peaceful reform of the Northern Ireland statelet became largely irrelevant in the light of an event such as Bloody Sunday. As Niall Ó Dochartaigh indicates, when government policy shifted from one of reform to one of repression, the alienation of Catholic moderates from the Northern state was one of the main results.[15] State repression and armed resistance seemed to have returned the conflict to the kind of political binary that had defined the very nature of the state itself. It is our belief that there was at the time the potential for a different way of thinking about the transformation of that particular society, but that Bloody Sunday acted to decisively limit the scope of viable alternatives to the *status quo ante*. It is our hope that this book may serve as a small contribution to such a process of questioning and imagining what possible futures there might be beyond the kinds of rigid thinking that produced Bloody Sunday in the first place.

The first chapter of this book locates Bloody Sunday in a social terrain of political and physical contest over the styles of governance and the legitimacy of the Northern Ireland statelet. The starting point is the demand for civil rights in relation to local elections, housing and policing, and the active campaigns that were launched to achieve them. The key idea in this chapter is that it was precisely the challenge posed by people in a movement against a sedentary state that saw such a vicious response to peaceful protesters by its police/militia and eventually by the army of its sponsor-state. Similarly, Free Derry posed an unambiguous challenge to the authority of the state and the rule of law across its domain. Those in charge of the military operation on 30 January 1972 have consistently argued that what was planned on the day was an arrest operation to 'scoop up' hard-core rioters who were engaged in constant harassment of troops positioned on the boundary of the Bogside. This notion of an arrest can be extended to encompass the broader effects of Bloody Sunday on the entire civil rights movement. The actions of the army on that day did not simply stop a protest parade reaching its intended target: it sounded the death knell for a fluid and dynamic process of social and political change, and the dialogic impulse at the heart of it.

The second chapter examines the ways in which photographs of the victims have been presented and manipulated in news media and commemorative events throughout the 35 years since Bloody Sunday. Tracing each moment at which the photographs have appeared, we argue that the deployment of the images by the families' campaigning groups produces a spectral effect: the images of the dead return in order to emphasise particular features of the Bloody Sunday story. We concentrate on the ways in which the victims' families' campaigns have deployed the faces of their loved ones as a powerful ethical reminder of this injustice. In this chapter we also look at the attempts of the Bogside Artists to commemorate Bloody Sunday and the broader civil rights movement through their 'People's Gallery' of murals.

The third chapter takes as its focus the 'technologies of truth' developed for and deployed within the new Bloody Sunday Inquiry. A central element of the Saville inquiry has been the development of a virtual-imaging environment to allow witnesses to navigate their way through the streets of the Bogside as they were in 1972. The reason for employing such a system is because the urban landscape of that part of Derry has, over the past three decades, changed out of all recognition: the present-day Bogside is a pleasant neighbourhood of flats and maisonettes, of striking murals and thriving community associations; the days of tiny overcrowded houses and multi-storey flats have long since disappeared. This impressive (and award-wining) virtual-Derry, designed by the Belfast-based Northern Ireland Centre for Learning Resources, has been hailed as a technological breakthrough. But what are the ethical implications underpinning such technological strategies of judicial inquiry? What issues are generated by placing virtual imaging at the very centre of an inquiry attempting to delineate a truthful version of events? The Bloody Sunday Inquiry has been the most technologically advanced judicial inquiry of its type: in addition to the virtual-imaging system, it has made use of other technologies (such as TrialPro – Evidence Display System and LiveNote – Real-Time Transcription) and live streaming to eight other locations in the Guildhall itself and a further four locations across Derry (the Calgach Centre, Rialto Theatre, Bloody Sunday Inquiry Office, and the former Bloody Sunday Trust offices on Shipquay Street). The inquiry has also made use of a dynamic website. Our chapter considers all of these technologies and their use as part of the truth-finding process.

The fourth chapter examines the 'reality strategies' employed in the two drama-documentaries released to coincide with the thirtieth anniversary of the killings: Paul Greengrass's *Bloody Sunday*, and Charles McDougall and Jimmy McGovern's *Sunday*. We find that these films share an overwhelming desire to present a version of events very much at odds with Lord Widgery's findings. These are films produced by 'outsiders' attempting to construct and articulate different aspects of what the journalist and political organiser Eamonn McCann refers to as the *moral* truth of Bloody Sunday.[16] The contrast in approaches adopted by the filmmakers raises important questions about the nature of attempting to construct an account that lays claim to reactivating the experiences of that day. While the desire to 'tell the story' may be entirely commendable (this is, after all, exactly what Mark Saville's inquiry is attempting to do), it is none the less notable that the films use certain rhetorical, stylistic, narratory and, indeed, sentimental conventions in order to achieve this aim. We detect in all representations a scrupulous conformity to what we term 'Bloody Sunday stylistics', in which certain photographic and filmic conventions established in television footage and photographic images on the afternoon of 30 January 1972 are deemed absolutely essential to all subsequent representations. When a film states unequivocally that what it presents to its audience is 'the truth', one begins to suspect a certain 'will to persuade' that presents several epistemological problems. This becomes even more acute when that film attempts to strengthen its monopoly of truth on the basis of its director's claims to have produced a version of events based to a large degree on the depth and extent of his embeddedness with the community and the people of the Bogside.

The fifth chapter takes as its focus Thomas Kinsella's ballad *Butcher's Dozen*. Written only days after Lord Widgery's report was published, Kinsella produces a dramatic poem in which the dead of Bloody Sunday appear to the poet in order to give their own testimony. Kinsella adapts the eighteenth-century gaelic *aisling*, or political dream poem, in his vivid portrayal of loss accompanied by an impassioned plea for truth and justice. Unlike other treatments of Bloody Sunday, *Butcher's Dozen* elaborates a politics of Bloody Sunday that sets the actions of the British Army on that day within a colonial framework.

The chapter looks at the ways in which Kinsella's poem is a necessary supplement to the Widgery Report, and it also considers the ethical issues provoked when a poet evokes the dead as memorialised remains, as spectres, or, indeed, as ventriloquised figures.

The sixth and final chapter looks at the ways in which Bloody Sunday has been negotiated through theatre. In this chapter we discuss the particular issues that come into play when cultural trauma is translated into forms of art and entertainment. The chapter takes a special interest in two theatrical works prompted by Bloody Sunday and its aftermath: Brian Friel's *The Freedom of the City* and Frank McGuinness's *Carthaginians*. Both plays attempt (in very different ways) to record the impact of the killings on individuals and the community of Derry. In discussing the plays' stylistics we are particularly concerned with how Friel and McGuinness (both of whom have strong associations with the city of Derry and its Donegal hinterland) deal with questions of memory, remembrance and communal trauma. We also briefly consider Richard Norton-Taylor's 2005 production, *Bloody Sunday: Scenes from the Saville Inquiry*, in which the many hundreds of witness statements given to the Saville inquiry are edited into a two-hour courtroom drama.

1

Turbulent Times
Bloody Sunday and
the Civil Rights Movement

There was a great air of excitement that day as I joined an immense throng
of neighbors, friends, and fellow nationalists in asserting our right to civil
disobedience. It was a beautiful sunny Sunday afternoon. I vividly recall
the blue sky, the cool fresh crispness in the Derry air, and the friendly
banter that turned the gathering into a near carnival.[1]

Introduction

There are many narratives of the 'Troubles' in Northern Ireland that
locate, describe and explain aspects of the diverse stories and experiences of those who lived through the conflict. In relation to the tragedy
of the lost lives perhaps the simplest yet most effective form of representation is the listing of those killed in Malcolm Sutton's *An Index of
Deaths from the Conflict in Northern Ireland 1969–1993* (1994) and in
David McKittrick's *Lost Lives*. Like Alan Clarke's film *Elephant* (1989),
the minimal approach communicates a powerful sense of the tragic
nature of the violence of those years. But an account of any one of those
events struggles with questions of establishing the parameters of what
material to include and exclude by way of establishing the particular
context of each act of violence. Similarly, in relation to Bloody Sunday,
the vast scale of the Saville inquiry illustrates the difficulties of establishing a narrative (and not simply a series of occurrences and processes
that may or may not concatenate into a version of events) that can be
credibly presented to all the parties involved. What can be perceived
about the period leading up to the event of Bloody Sunday is that it was
one marked by particular tendencies at work within the social realm. In
the same way that it is impossible to plot every change of pressure or
direction in all the elements of a hurricane, it is impossible to identify
every element of the period of intense social turmoil and uncertainty of
Northern Ireland in the 1960s and '70s. But it is possible to identify
certain movements and social pressures that shaped the environment
and that can be presented as providing a useful conceptual frame to help

11

explain why that society took the direction it did at that time. A key vector of the call for social configuration was the broad demand for civil rights that spanned issues of voting, living conditions, policing and justice. Bloody Sunday marked a qualitative change in popular nationalist attitudes towards the state and the relationship to that state of a part of society most directly concerned with confronting (and changing the discriminatory nature of) those issues.

What we seek to do in this opening chapter, therefore, is to provide an understanding of the period immediately prior to Bloody Sunday. A significant characteristic of the period was that it was one rich in the belief in the possibility of fundamental social change that could have gone in any number of directions. What follows is an attempt to productively integrate theoretical concepts that provide a useful understanding of both structure and agency, neither of which are ever static or simply dominant. This is not an attempt to reduce the complexity of a particular human society down to some sort of mechanical process that denies the role of intentional agents. However, it is a rejection of the sort of thinking that defines actions or actors in crudely simplistic terms from one side of a moral binary or in relation to an imaginary origin. The philosopher Manuel Delanda articulates the need for a 'nonlinear' history, defined as one that pays proper attention to the density and complex nature of different structures within any given system. In this way, there is nothing inevitable in such systems and they do not move progressively in a unilinear direction. He writes of the need to develop a methodology true to the nature of the interactive elements under analysis:

> Specifically, we need to take into account that any explanation of human behaviour must involve reference to irreducible intentional entities such as 'beliefs' and 'desires', since expectations and preferences are what guide human decision making in a wide range of social activities, such as politics and economics. In some cases the decisions made by individual human beings are highly constrained by their position and role in a hierarchical organization and are, to that extent, geared toward meeting the goals of that organization. In other cases, however, what matters is not the planned results of decision making, but the *unintended collective consequences* of human decisions.[2]

What becomes apparent with any reading of the witness statements of residents and protesters who set out on the march in Derry on that day in 1972 was the sense of community and solidarity present within the large, multi-faceted crowd that assembled at Creggan shops in order to challenge the crude terror of state violence represented by internment without trial. As Don Mullan recounts in the epigraph, there was a carnival-like atmosphere amongst the crowd that wended its way down towards the city centre. What this atmosphere suggests is the complex nature of the struggle amongst the people at that time to force change from the unionist regime: it is clear from Mullan's statement (and from the testimony of many others present on the march) that, whilst driven by a deep sense of injustice and anger, the event also had elements of humour and joyfulness about it. What we mean by this is not some notion of innocent playfulness; these were, after all, people who were well aware of the reaction of the RUC and the British Army to such unrest, but rather to the expansive feeling that comes from becoming active in the struggle to resist the limitations imposed by a rigid and oppressive state. It is this quality that we relate to Mikhail Bakhtin's concept of the carnival, with its linking of imagination, desire and resistance. This moment of collective refusal of the sovereign edict can be best described as a form of minor-politics, to use a term deriving from Deleuze and Guattari.[3] Being literally and figuratively confined, the defiance of those that day was driven by multiple motivations reflecting the complex nature of such communities; there were no simple answers to the problems at hand and disagreements and tensions between the elements within the protesting crowd were clearly manifest. So we begin by considering the demand for civil rights as a movement, before looking at Free Derry as an expression of resistance defined by the limits of a bounded space and ultimately Bloody Sunday as bringing together those concepts of movement and space and the attempt to halt this process and reclaim space for the state. The analysis offered here is informed by Delanda's notion of a 'geological ethics', where the energy directed at the destratification of hardened institutions offers the possibility for self-organisation not predicated on coercion or conflict.[4]

Civil rights *movement*

First, we want to consider what is referred to as the civil rights movement as a collection of affiliated campaigns and individuals, the key aspect of which was precisely that it was engaged in a strategy of 'movement' rather than the formal notion of an organisation. Emerging from a number of campaigns launched throughout the mid- to late 1960s, such as the Campaign for Social Justice, and the Northern Ireland Civil Rights Association, through to locally based housing and anti-unemployment campaigns, the movement sought to force reform from the unionist state which had ruled for fifty years on the basis of systematic discrimination and political manipulation. As a broad-based movement it contained any number of disparate political ideologies, from reformism informed by Catholicism through to the revolutionary claims of Maoism, and in this sense its polyvocality articulated the Bakhtinian sense of optimism and becoming. Its central aims were, however, clearly enough understood and agreed upon: to bring an end to discrimination in employment and housing allocation, and to compel the government of Northern Ireland to bring about fundamental changes in the areas of voting, policing and the justice system. As might be expected from its nomenclature, non-violent direct action was the key strategy with which to confront the state. But the defining strength of the civil rights movement lay in its demand for legal and constitutional rights *within* the state in the first instance. Traditionally, resistance to the Northern Irish state had resided in republicanism, which denied the legitimacy of the statelet itself, counter-posing, rather, a 'United Ireland' as the singular aspiration. But whilst there is no doubt that within the civil rights movement such an aspiration was present, it was not an organising principle as such.

Most importantly, the civil rights movement aspired to work beyond the defining category of the state itself, which was that of religion. The binary coding of sectarian dualism of Protestant and Catholic described the social and political machinery of Northern Ireland. Not surprisingly, those who supported the state vehemently challenged the movement as nothing other than a front for violent republicanism, and, indeed, as a political strategy it had a profoundly destabilising effect upon a state that was unwilling (though by no means unable) to move beyond its organising religious principles:

> The civil rights campaign had disrupted the balance of power in Northern Ireland by the simple fact of mobilisation of the Catholic community. It was not so much that Northern Ireland could not be reformed. By the summer of 1969, it already had been reformed to some extent. It was that it could not incorporate its Catholic minority into the political process. It could not offer Catholics the prospect of political power.[5]

This strategy of destratification[6] shook the state to its foundations: in other words, to its founding political and conceptual principles. The civil rights movement was not seeking the dismantling of the Northern Irish state as such (even if elements within it would have been more than happy to see this), rather, an immanent process of decoding and deterri-torialisation worked to operate upon the foundational terms of social and political organisation to intensify the effect of refusing those terms at the same time as working with them. Bob Purdie writes:

> The new strategy was inspired by the Black civil rights movement in the United States. The term 'civil rights' had not been used to define the aspirations of the minority community in Northern Ireland before the 1960s and it had never before adopted a strategy that was both militant and constitutional.[7]

The intention, therefore, was not to produce chaos, in the sense of anarchic disruption, but to pose relations that could not be contained within the existing social and political organisation of Northern Ireland. The conjunction of the demand for civil rights for the minority within a sectarian state produced a violent response driven by prejudice and incomprehension. It would be wrong to characterise the civil rights movement at this time in singular terms; it was by definition a loose affiliation of disparate campaigns and politics that were generally antagonistic towards each other. But it drew a fairly consistent response from the state: mainly outright refusal of its demands or, at best, reluctant concession, coupled with large-scale repression. At this point the activities of the civil rights movement shift away from the notion of a licensed event, one of the limitations of Bakhtin's notion of the carnival, to one of becoming increasingly confrontational.

The civil rights movement in Northern Ireland drew inspiration from the US Black civil rights movement and other areas of social collectivity that defined the optimistic and speculative nature of the period.[8] Of course, there were many differences between them, but the strategy of non-violent protest was central to both, as was the aggressive and violent response of the local state and its police. A crucial element for both movements, therefore, was the generation of new circuits of resistance through the transmission of television images of brutal suppression of peaceful marches.[9] Gerry Murray, a resident of the Creggan estate in Derry, articulates the relationships between the local and the global:

> Before the year was over, Derry was destined to appear on television screens across the world. The first marches for civil rights were eagerly grasped by our parents, anxious to see a better future for us in terms of jobs, housing and the ability to control the destiny of our city. The famous words uttered five years earlier by Martin Luther King, 'I have a dream', had a powerful meaning for our parents and symbolised their determination to see wrongs put right. There was a great sense of unity of purpose and a lack of dissent. The politics of non-violence and the songs of the American Civil Rights movement were readily embraced in the spirit of hope and determination.[10]

The image of the Westminster MP Gerry Fitt being viciously struck by a baton-wielding RUC officer on Duke Street on 5 October 1968 has become iconic of such moments. More importantly it, and other images of brutality against peaceful protestors, served to mobilise Catholics and supporters of civil rights across the north and south of Ireland. The role of television images was not lost on the campaigners from that point on. The response of the state, especially the police, forced an escalation of the protestors' actions, causing no small amount of anguish for the middle-class and liberal-inclined sections of the movement. As Purdie writes:

> The launching of street marches by the Northern Ireland Civil Rights Association (NICRA) in 1968 could be seen as a logical consequence of the closure of every other channel to bring about reform, but it divided the Liberals.[11]

The problem for, in Purdie's term, the 'Liberals' was that it was going to be relatively easy to get people onto the streets but not so easy to get them off again. The shift in strategy to organised marches in protest was a significant one.

To march for civil rights was a point of connection with an international tradition of social protest, but it also connected with a tradition rather more internal to Northern Ireland itself: sectarian parades. To walk, to march, to parade, involves many aspects of cultural and symbolic power: movement across territory is something vigorously policed by the modern state. Freedom of movement in the modern state is essentially an illusion. One is not simply free to walk in the middle of the road, for instance, because the economic imperative of vehicular traffic flow takes precedence. The concept of private property asserts the right to exclude others from crossing one's sovereign territory. A complex system of legal and political prohibitions works, therefore, to closely supervise such practices.[12] To march across territory requires the charitable acquiescence of the police to such an event, and will be subject to close supervision and summary changes if it is deemed excessively disruptive to the functioning of daily life. However, the normative parameters of 'daily life' are not abstract relationships but depend entirely upon the political contours of the local environment. Within Northern Ireland this could be seen (and it is an inherently visual display) in the tradition of Orange Order parades.

Neil Jarman writes of the way in which the strategy of marching for civil rights impacted upon the cultural environment of Northern Ireland, where the 'right to march' had been central to the loyalist tradition of parading. As he says: 'While the use of protest marches was drawn from the example of the American civil rights movement, it confronted head-on the loyalist belief that parading was largely the prerogative of Unionists'.[13] The civil rights marches were therefore as contentious as any explicitly political demand. They exposed the power lines of the sectarian state and the social order that it had been able to maintain as normative. As Jarman states:

> For while the loyalists insisted on their inalienable right to parade wherever and whenever they wished, this right was not extended to Catholics. Civil rights parades did not fit into the traditional polarities; but by challenging the authority of the Protestant state and demanding equal rights for the minority they became immediately liable to be categorised as Catholic and nationalist.[14]

Further, it can be argued that it was precisely the carnivalesque potential at work within civil rights marches that also distinguished them from Orange Order parades as they actively sought to invert dominant social relations. As Jack Santino points out, the rigid and hierarchical nature of officially-sanctioned parades acts as a containment of the challenging potential of the carnival and articulates a reinforcing of social power: 'The Derry [Apprentice Boys] parades and Orange parades reinforce hierarchy while suspending some prohibitions. While they partake partially in the carnivalesque, their intention is to inscribe hegemony upon territory'.[15] Jarman similarly distinguishes between the open and informal aspects of the republican parades as opposed to the triumphal and militarised nature of the loyalist tradition.[16]

At this point we want to relate the carnivalesque and open aspects of civil rights protests to some of the ideas articulated by Paul Virilio in his book *Speed and Politics*. For Virilio such marches have been perceived as an 'ambulatory manifestation' of the revolutionary potential of the masses.[17] He identifies the destabilising aspect of this as one of acceleration. This is a powerful concept with which to recognise the revolutionary potential of the civil rights movement. People in movement, ways of thinking in movement, a state forced into movement: all of these things are true, but of course they are also always already in movement. It is not movement in the abstract but movement that seeks new ways of thinking, of acting, of imagining, that is potentially revolutionary. It is the fact that what is being challenged are the ways in which the state seeks to control movement that is significant. As stated above, marching was a central element to the dominant identity of the unionist state, but when the minor seeks to traverse the terrain of the major a very different potential comes into play. Parading continues to be the primary means by which to express collective identities and claim dominance over territory[18] and a central element of negotiating peace in the province has been an 'independent' commission to rule on contentious marches.

Containment had been a key aspect of the control of local and state power within Northern Ireland. Derry, most significantly, had remained a unionist-controlled city because of the strict maintenance of electoral ward boundaries and the curtailing of new house building in religiously-mixed areas. A central demand of the civil rights movement had been for universal suffrage in local government elections (reluctantly conceded in 1969). Voting in Northern Ireland until then had been dependent upon one being a rate-payer and anomalies also meant that companies had multiple votes. It was possible for a company owner to have a number of votes whilst a family that included several adults but living in rented accommodation had only the one. Whilst clearly favouring one class over another (and so cutting across the binary of religious identity), it also points to the profoundly sedentary basis of the state, which is to refuse to recognise a body as eligible for political power unless it begins to re-conceptualise the terms of its relationship to the land: to be an elector one must be a property owner. As we will see, the danger posed by the march of 30 January 1972 was a danger of turbulence within the field of social movement, of circulating outside the parameters of the very terms by which the Northern Irish statelet conceptualised itself: terms that were posited as rigid, eternal and identical. Deleuze and Guattari write of the dynamic nature of the nomadic potential that operates at the margins and is fundamentally metamorphic:

> In short, we will say by convention that only nomads have absolute movement, in other words, speed; vortical or swirling movement is an essential feature of their war machine.[19]

We will consider this further when looking at the march of 30 January itself.

Free Derry

Free Derry was 'thrown up' in 1969 in response to concerted attacks on the Bogside by the police and their auxiliary reserve force, the infamous B-Specials, a force renowned for its brutality and mobilised almost exclusively against the Catholic minority. Paddy Docherty articulates well the fact that the creation of a ghetto is an easy way to contain and manage a minority, but it has a paradoxical relationship to state power in that it can switch to become a well-defined and defendable site of resistance:

> Free Derry encompassed the Bogside, the sprawling Creggan housing estate, the more compact Brandywell and a small middle-class area. The territory held by the rebels roughly corresponded to the South Ward, which had been set up by the Unionist administration to contain the Catholic population of the city. The newly liberated territory measured 888 acres and two roods, or roughly one and a half square miles. By gerrymandering the city for over half a century, the Unionists had inadvertently created an Achilles heel for themselves. Twenty-eight thousand despised people shoved together, piled on top of each other and discriminated against, had decided that enough was enough. They were now outside the law, and their position, energy, and numbers posed a threat to the very existence of the state.[20]

Drawing its nomenclature from Free Berkeley in the USA, Free Derry quickly established itself as a zone of autonomy where the police and loyalists were physically repelled and kept back behind hastily erected barricades that, over time, became more permanent. This phrase 'Free Derry' is suggestive of Hakim Bey's most famous work, *The Temporary Autonomous Zone*, in which he argues that a potential exists at the boundaries of established order for new formations to emerge that elude formal control. Self-generated structures of communication and new networks of information can form temporary spaces outside the fixed hierarchies of the established order: a process that is, as Bey argues, inherently creative. The concept usefully draws attention to the tendency of any system to develop structures of permanence that inevitably begin to contain the creative and radical energies that had created it.[21] For some, Bey's concept challenges aspects of Bakhtin's notion of the carnival, because it refuses to engage with the state in any way and cannot, therefore, be appropriated. However, it is important to recognise Free Derry as an act of self-defence, generated by its inhabitants' justified fears of state-sanctioned brutality, arson and murder. Like the monument to it, 'Free Derry' was of, yet simultaneously after, the act. The initial assertion of the space was a creative response to the problems posed by the reaction of the forces of the state to the demands for civil rights.

The establishing of Free Derry gave physical manifestation to the already-existing processes of minor-becoming at work within the Northern Irish statelet discussed above. But it was, of course, a process in which many contradictory forces were working. Eamonn McCann articulates most clearly the 'swirling' nature of the time, where all ideas were open to debate and power was distributed throughout the mass of people all actively participating in the resistance: 'the chaos we felt around us was for real, and rich in possibilities other than those which came to pass' and at that time 'no political tendency had hegemony'.[22] The constitution of Free Derry was, therefore, driven by the need to defend a space and yet to move beyond the physical boundaries that defined it. Paul Patton writes of the quite different relationships to space posed by the contrasting conceptualisations of the understanding of territory:

> In contrast to the roads and highways that connect the regions of sedentary space, the paths of nomadic existence serve to distribute individuals and groups across an open and indeterminate space. Whereas sedentary space is striated by enclosures and paths between enclosures, the territory of nomadic peoples is a pure surface for mobile existence, without enclosures or fixed patterns of distribution.[23]

Free Derry was a social entity that was fundamentally exterior to the Northern Irish state; this was the danger it posed. Its exteriority co-existed with interiority in a competing terrain defined by what escapes the state.[24] For the RUC and, subsequently, the British Army it was a 'no-go' zone, where the concept of law was something other than that defined by state power. Yet to the people who lived within it, it was, at the same time, a thoroughly permeable space. It was not a utopian space in an idealised sense, as the reading of any account written by those who lived there makes clear. What is evident is the constraining nature of existence for those in Free Derry. The notion of minor is intrinsically linked to the confronting of boundaries and limits to that which is in movement. Yet, as Thoburn observes, the 'impossibility' of action is mirrored by the impossibility of passivity 'if anything is to be lived'.[25]

What Free Derry did was to manifest the refusal of the subjected minority to accept the legitimacy of both the violence of the state and its right to exercise violence through its agents. Such a space is intolerable to the state, which is driven by the need to colonise, capture and regulate the processes of lived experience. The externality of Free Derry posed a profoundly antipathetic mode of existence to the Northern Irish statelet and, by extension, to the British state. The process of reaction generated by the state leading up to and beyond Bloody Sunday can, arguably, be seen as a concerted attempt to reduce the dynamic and multiple nature of this political and social formation to another kind of binary: that of a militarised conflict occurring in a heavily striated space.[26] This imperative manifests itself directly on the day of the march on 30 January 1972.

Bloody Sunday

As part of its strategy of repression and containment of the threat posed to it by the emergent reality of armed republicanism, the unionist government had introduced internment without trial in August 1971. The march of 30 January 1972 was envisaged by the Northern Ireland Civil Rights Association (NICRA) as the largest protest yet against this injustice. As the level of protest escalated, so all marches had been banned. The march that day had therefore been designated as illegal and the route to the Guildhall Square in the centre of Derry was blocked at several points by army barriers. The organisers responded by reluctantly re-routing the march past the closed-off streets and directing the parade back into the heart of the Bogside in order to hold the rally at Free Derry Corner.

What becomes apparent from this point onward is a conflict of perception of what was in process. As Delanda observes, whether we view the demographic pressures which impact upon warfare as 'creative' or 'destructive' will depend on our point of view.[27] There is a strongly held view amongst many commentators on Northern Ireland that the primary effect of Bloody Sunday was to mark the end of the civil rights strategy of non-violent direct action and the concomitant growth of both latent acceptance and manifest support amongst nationalists for the armed campaign of the Provisional IRA. Bloody Sunday was one of a number of key events that served as a defining trauma in a collective community sense and as a moment of conversion on an individual basis for many of those involved. This connected and made concrete the micro and the macro levels of conflict where the defining parameters of normality were shattered by a violent act.[28] Given the recognition by many of this incident as the one that effected a fundamental shift in the

relationship between Catholics and the state and was crucial in esca-
lating the militarisation of the conflict, it could be characterised as a
'threshold event'. Most commonly, a threshold event refers to the impact
of a factor that changes a body from one state to another, for instance a
liquid changing to a solid. Such a formulation suggests that there is
another way of thinking about Bloody Sunday and its context.

It should be clear that a conflict situation such as this was highly
complex, contingently open-ended, and that a range of possible futures
could have been generated. For these reasons the characterisation of the
situation as complex is a reference to complexity theory, an example of
what John Urry calls 'the complexity turn'.[29] This range of disciplinary
transformations is characterised by an awareness of the complex and
open nature of systems that have a transformational potential. At any
one time such systems are in balance between order and chaos and,
counter to dominant thinking, do not necessarily tend towards equilibrium. As David Byrne states, 'Complexity science is inherently
dynamic'.[30] The advantage such thinking offers for conflict scenarios is
worth considering further. Indeed, William Cunningham has written of
the usefulness of this approach specifically to Northern Ireland:

> The reason that we turn to chaos and complexity theories in conflict
> analysis and resolution is that it offers novel and interesting ways to
> analyze the behaviour of dynamic systems. In human social life there
> are few processes or systems that are as dynamic or complex as con-
> flict systems.[31]

This approach allows us to attempt to appreciate the active relationship
between agency and deterministic laws in these scenarios.

Accounts of the march on 30 January 1972 consistently paint a
picture of a large crowd peacefully marching down into the Bogside.
The flow of thousands of people was dammed by army barricades
manned by soldiers at two key points into the city centre. The flat-
backed coal lorry carrying the organisers turned back into the Bogside
to avoid the confrontation, and stewards attempted to marshal people
away from the points of contact with the army and police. However,
through a mixture of confusion and frustration (and, it must be said,
ritualised behaviour) a minor riot situation developed at the foot of
William Street. This can be characterised as a point of turbulence. The
relatively stable flow of marchers became less so and from one point of
view would have seemed chaotic. As the situation developed, the per-
ceptions of those involved begin to diverge at an exponential rate.
McCann and others describe the ebb and flow of a familiar process of
moving towards soldiers and police with a barrage of rocks and the
standard response of CS gas, water cannon and rubber bullets in a form
of elemental warfare. For the army commanders the rioting is perceived
as organised by key individuals; for the rioters and observers there is no

such distinction as marchers joined in and then perhaps withdrew from the immediate area of conflict. A sense of unity and community can be identified among the crowd, which is not simply an aggregate of individuals, but an open and dynamic entity operating through a bodily register and located outside the official discourse. Bakhtin writes of the crowd in this way:

> The carnivalesque crowd in the marketplace or in the streets is not merely a crowd. It is the people as a whole, but organised *in their own way*, the way of the people. It is outside of and contrary to all existing forms of the coercive socioeconomic and political organization, which is suspended for the time of the festivity.[32]

As Stallybrass and White point out, it is important not to essentialise carnival as inherently radical, but at the same time what can be said is that, 'given the presence of sharpened political antagonism, it may often act as catalyst and site of actual and symbolic struggle'.[33]

The key to understanding the next stage of the army action can be traced to a memo dictated by General Ford in which he articulates the need to identify and shoot leaders of the 'Derry Young Hooligans'. The young men of the area are to be the target of soldiers using low-velocity bullets in specially adapted rifles. Such a strategy is predicated upon the notion that there is a small group, a few hundred strong at most, who organise themselves to engage in attacks upon the army and police. Accounts of the time indicate that for many young men a culture of confrontation and property destruction had established itself, much to the annoyance of more conservative Catholics.[34] Nevertheless, for the army there was no concept of a community mobilising itself in diverse and multiple ways to resist the constraining and offensive nature of military occupation. For the armed men working at the behest of the state, those to be targeted are defined by a specific identity such as 'hooligan' and as such they are intrinsically connected to the real enemy, the 'terrorists' for whom they are perceived to provide cover.

Once there is a perceptible separation between the different layers of the crowd (in other words between 'peaceful' marchers and so-called 'hooligans'), the order is given to allow the paratroopers to move forwards to engage in an arrest operation. It is clear from all accounts that it is at this point – the movement of the Paras into the Bogside – that the events that we think of as constituting 'Bloody Sunday' become virtually inevitable. In the language of complexity theory, this moment can be understood as a bifurcation: a change in the qualitative nature of the attractor, where the attractor can be defined as the state or point towards which a system tends.[35] From this point onwards, the range of possible outcomes is greatly reduced. Changes in key variables generate social changes as a process of polarisation.[36] Such points allow for a pattern to be identified and a solution to be plotted: by initiating overwhelming aggressive military action the variables were inevitably condensed around violence. Cunningham articulates why such a concept can be useful in this analysis:

> Bifurcations are important to understanding system behaviour at the edge of chaos – between order and disorder. Decisions that are made, for instance whether to call a cease-fire or continue a violent campaign, are highly important to determine the path of chaotic systems. This is one of the reasons that chaos theory is important to conflict resolution.[37]

Bifurcation events are the critical point at which there is a profound change in the attractor. In general, through a certain range of changes in values the attractors will change only subtly, but at this critical point there is a transformation.[38]

It is precisely at such a moment that attractors offer different possibilities for the long-term behaviour of the system. One incident can potentially transform the long-term trajectory of the entire system. On the wider scale of conflict in Northern Ireland, Bloody Sunday was not necessarily the most significant event but, arguably, was one of a small number of points from which the subsequent system-wide pattern was generated. The relevance of complexity theory is precisely that although the input change may not seem relatively unusual, the outcome effect is enormous:

> One state is replaced by another through a non-linear transformation which is nonetheless singular. There is only one new state possible. Chaotic transformations are not really about states or steady conditions. Rather they are about trajectories, about the dynamic development of systems. The connection is the idea of *bifurcation* which describes the development of very different system trajectories in consequence of very small variations in the values of initial conditions. The usual form of chaotic attractor which is most described is the *Lorenz* or *butterfly* attractor.[39]

Certainly the trajectory of the movement to challenge the system subsequent to Bloody Sunday was very different from that that went before. On the day itself the focus of the commanding officer on the ground was defined in terms of the task at hand, which is to isolate the incident from any wider system of analysis. This approach reflects the traditional approach within science to artificially isolate systems to analyse them, in the belief that they will achieve a steady-state equilibrium. What is ignored, therefore, is any notion that there is a much more dynamic process at work. Subsequently, for General Ford the military intervention of 30 January 1972 had been deemed a success because, as he is reported to have said that Sunday night, 'Londonderry is quiet'. This reference to the stilling of the 'noise' of the subject population is indicative of a perception of the threat posed by the crowd and, by extension, the troublesome community as one of disturbance/turbulence, what Michel Serres describes as 'an arborescent and turbulent rumor'.[40]

Once the order was given to go into the Bogside, soldiers entered in armoured vehicles driven at high speed towards the crowd. This highlights the central strategy of the armed policing of the different zones within Northern Ireland that was beginning to emerge at this point. Virilio usefully articulates the centrality of the ability to move quickly for the armies of the state:

> Speed is the hope of the West; it is speed that supports the armies' morale. What 'makes war convenient' is transportation, and the armoured car, able to go over every kind of terrain, erases the obstacles.[41]

For the paratroopers, the ability to penetrate into the heart of the Bogside was dependent on the fast and protective shell of the Saracen armoured vehicles, or 'pigs' as they tended to be called by the soldiers. No longer within the domain of water or gas, hard metal is used as a projectile against the soft tissue of bodies. The 'pigs' are projectiles fired into the body of the Bogside before individual soldiers spill out onto the ground, adopt firing positions and fire bullets into the fleeing crowds.

It is useful to contrast the different vehicular strategies of the combatants within the Northern Irish conflict. The British Army had all-terrain high-speed armoured cars, a cross between a Land Rover and a tank. The guerrilla forces of the IRA 'hijacked' cars and travelled with weapons stored in the boot. One of the key developments of the permanent surveillance state that Northern Ireland became over the twenty years after Bloody Sunday was the use of number-plate recognition software to identify and track suspected IRA movements. If the revolution takes place on the street, then the ability to move quickly becomes a key determinant of political power. Virilio's thesis is that the essence of revolution is speed, as he writes, making specific reference to Northern Ireland:

> After Belfast, Beirut showed us the old communal city crushed under the blows of the Palestinian migrants. What they lived through was not the old state of siege, but an aimless and permanent state of emergency. To survive in the city one had to stay informed daily, by radio, about the strategic situation of one's own neighborhood; everyone transformed his car into an assault vehicle, loaded with weapons in order to ensure freedom of movement.[42]

Six months after Bloody Sunday, and in the aftermath of 'Bloody Friday', when the IRA blitzed the centre of Belfast causing widespread death and destruction, the code word for the smashing of the barricades of Free Derry and the reclaiming for the state of the no-go zones was 'Operation Motorman', a term that conflates the human with the technologies of speed mobilised by the state to crush dissent.

What becomes apparent are the different tendencies at work in the instigation of Bloody Sunday: the strategies of containment, control and fixed points of order employed by the army and state against ever-adapting processes of social transformation employed by those associated with the civil rights movement. This does not offer a simple binary between the two; we characterise them instead as tendencies. Within the civil rights movement there was an inherent conservatism (change but not too much too fast, epitomised by the influence of the Catholic Church) and at the same time elements of the military machine, aware of the need for the adoption of guerrilla tactics (mobile undercover assassination squads in unmarked cars). What is evident, however, is the non-linear nature of the event. For Cunningham, the concept of the fractal is pertinent to the complexity of a conflict situation such as Northern Ireland. The irregular, geometrical shapes are infinitely self-generating and self-similar at all levels:

> This self-similarity at all scales is important because it illustrates the presence of chaos theory and nonlinearity on all levels: the individual, group, societal, international, and global. Each fractal has the same shapes and qualities at all scales and levels.[43]

By considering such conflict scenarios through the application of complexity theory, a different way of thinking, beyond the binaries of conventional thought, are suggested. The disruptive nature of working at the boundary between order and chaos cannot be simply restrained by the force of either military or state thinking.

In tracing the different moments of self-organising and strategies of becoming at work in the civil rights movement of Northern Ireland of the late 1960s and '70s, it is possible to see how the conflict involved quite different conceptualisations of social order, dissent and transformation. To consider Bloody Sunday in this way is to reject the singularising tendency of the official inquiry of Lord Saville. The concept of the carnivalesque is at heart a process that is responsive to the porous nature of the encounters at work in a movement such as this and communicates the sense of a vibrant oscillation between the poles of doubt and certainty that, in turn, generate an openness characterised by a type of humour and joy.[44] Bloody Sunday replaced that with anger and an enduring bitterness, and a much-reduced sense of the potential for social reconfiguration beyond the structures of thinking driven by the past rather than possible futures.

The thinking behind the army's intervention can be characterised as the repressive instincts of a colonial mindset where the desired effect is one of sustaining a system defined in mechanical terms: static, fixed and linear. In contrast, the key aspect of the civil rights movement as it came into being was its orientation towards change, flux and speculative intervention. The dialogic impulse at work in the movement was drastically slowed, if not immediately halted, by the act of calculated state violence carried out on 30 January 1972 in Derry.

2
Faces of the Dead
Photography, Commemoration, Campaign

The cult of remembrance of loved ones, absent or dead, offers a last refuge for the cult value of the picture. For the last time the aura emanates from the early photographs in the fleeting expression of the human face.[1]

The face is not a force. It is an authority.[2]

[It] 'is what resists me by its opposition and not what is opposed to me by its resistance. . . . The absolute nakedness of a face, the absolutely defenceless face, without covering, clothing or mask, is what opposes my power over it, my violence, and opposes it in an absolute way, with an opposition which is opposition itself.[3]

Introduction

Our starting-point in this chapter is the portrait photographs of the men and boys killed on Bloody Sunday. These images of the faces of the dead were central to the news reports of the massacre and went on to become a central element in the different campaigns, initiated within the community and amongst the families, for truth and justice. Through the different mobilisations, translations and presentations, they became iconic images, expressions of the enduring injustice this event came to represent in the minds of those affected. In this sense, therefore, what is at work is, on the one hand, an act of mourning, an expression of loss through the continuous return to the indexical traces of loved ones irretrievably lost through the actions of the British Army. But they have also moved beyond that to become actively mobilised as part of a *demand* for action made by the campaigns to the British government on all aspects of the events leading up to and during that day.

These are not official mugshots of the criminal or the wanted, they are faces of those killed by a violent act, a violence that is extended to the photographic trace itself as it is incised from its private context and transferred into the grid of the mediatised public domain. Since the days following the killings the portraits have been deployed in a number of ways, each time reflecting changing concerns among the families and the

27

groups campaigning on their behalf, and each time producing quite distinct rhetorical effects and ethical demands. The notion of rhetoric will be central to our argument that the displaying and parading of the photographs is not just an act of commemoration or of mourning, but is in fact a critical intervention – an act of persuasion – in the campaign to force the British government to officially recognise the innocence of those killed and to establish the truth behind the circumstances of what happened. The rhetorical deployment of the portrait images did not, in fact, come to an end with the setting up of the Saville Inquiry. Carried by the victims' relatives on the annual Bloody Sunday marches, situated at key points in the city of Derry and beyond it, and transformed into the minor-monumental form of the street mural, the photographs continue to influence the debate concerning Bloody Sunday. They continue to function as a form of apostrophe, as an instance of epideictic speech, as a demonstrative utterance that carries suggestions of blame. And because they are instances of direct address to the living by the dead, they are also powerful instances of prosopopoeia, in which the absent or the dead urge the living to action. It is the process whereby essentially private photographs became transformed into iconic signifiers of the demand for justice that we explore in this chapter.

Strange meeting

We begin with the first moment of collective representation of those killed on Bloody Sunday. Reports of the killings (including large-format photographs of the paratroopers entering the Bogside, of brutally executed arrests, of victims being attended to by Knights of Malta paramedics and by their fellow marchers) appeared in most of the British and Irish Monday-morning newspapers. But it was not until the following day, Tuesday 1 February 1972, that the portrait photographs of the dead were featured. Indeed, not every British and Irish national newspaper carried the images. Many, including the regional daily evening newspaper the *Belfast Telegraph*, featured dramatic photographs of the events but not the 'portraits' themselves. The newspapers that did carry the portraits of the dead men arranged the images in a cellular structure composing a grid, although with differences in arrangement. For example, under the headline 'The Thirteen who Died on Bloody Sunday', the *Derry Journal* featured photographs of twelve victims, whilst reserving a larger-format image of Willie McKinney to illustrate a brief feature on his work as a printer on the paper. Entitled 'Our Colleague is Dead', the feature told its readers:

> Willie was not a stone-thrower, a bomber or a gunman. He had gone to the Civil Rights march in the role of amateur photographer. He was a printer to trade, an outstanding craftsman; the lay-out of some

of the reports and advertisements in this very issue, which also records his untimely death, bear testimony to his professional ability.

The *Irish News* (Belfast), meanwhile, presented the photographs in two rows between the masthead and the headline 'Nation to Honour Derry 13'. Under each image, arranged in a different order to the *Derry Journal*, appeared the name, age, street and neighbourhood of each victim. Some of the men's occupations were given: 'Gerald Donaghey [*sic*] (17), labourer, Meehan Square; Gerald McKinney (35), traveller, Knockdarragh Flats, Waterside.' There was a mix-up between the captions under the photographs of William Nash and James Wray. Giving prominence in their leading article to the reaction of the Irish government, the paper's coverage was uniformly critical of the British Army's actions and sceptical towards official British explanations of those actions: the testimony of seven priests, all of whom were eyewitnesses to the events, was a crucial part of the paper's front-page coverage. The *Irish News*'s approach was markedly similar to that of Tuesday's edition of *The Irish Times* (Dublin), which, again, featured the photographs in two rows, under the headline 'The 13 Shot Dead at Bogside Rally'. The treatment given the images by *The Times* (London) was the most impressive of all the newspapers on that day. A double-page spread was devoted to a range of eyewitness accounts, journalists' reports, transcripts of television news programmes and press-conference proceedings. The dead were represented in two rows under the headline 'We were holding white hankies in the air but the army opened up on us, witness says'. The witness in question was Anthony Martin, a former member of the Royal Navy and the Ulster Defence Regiment; his testimony featured prominently alongside other eyewitness accounts of the shootings. The following day the paper featured eyewitness accounts of five of the wounded, all of them photographed in various states of distress in their Altnagelvin hospital beds. Other means of representing the trauma of the day included a cartoon on the front page of the *Guardian* (Manchester and London) with the caption 'Giant's Causeway'. In the illustration the famous rock formation on the northern coastline of County Antrim is constructed of thirteen upturned coffins with a negotiating table perched atop the highest coffin. The *Daily Telegraph* (London) did not use the portrait images, but its 2 February edition carried, like several other British newspapers, a photograph of thirteen crosses being placed on the steps of the RUC barracks in the small town of Dungiven in County Derry alongside a photograph of a British soldier bowing his head in observance of a minute's silence: this was an image that was carried (no doubt for ameliorative purposes) by several British newspapers. As for the British tabloids, the *Daily Record* (Glasgow) devoted most of a page to the portraits, with the dual headline, 'They fell on Bloody Sunday' and 'Was there a Blunder?' And while not featuring the images, the *Sun*'s

Figure I. *The Irish News* front page, Monday, 1 February 1972 *(Photo courtesy of Noel Doran, Editor, The Irish News)*

(London) front page on Monday 31 January carried the headline 'The Bloody Sunday "Massacre"'.

It is no great surprise that the dead were represented by photographs of their faces, nor that those images were arranged in the form of a grid. As John Tagg argues, the use of a portrait by newspapers is an attempt to anchor an account of a dramatic event by illustrating it with a representation of its 'human face', on the assumption that the face is expressive of the truth of the subject.[4] The configuration of the individual photographs in the grid formation allows the distinct elements of the event to be presented in a singular, immediately graspable, context. Looking across the various newspapers' arrangements of the images-within-grids, a number of similarities and differences can be identified. Although there is an attempt to impose uniformity, the variations in size, quality and ordering within the grid insist on an irreducible difference. The grid may suggest, or impose, a certain uniformity, but the material that constitutes it, the thirteen individual photographs, insists upon a somewhat different register: these images of variable quality derive not from manifestly official sources, such as criminal mugshots, surveillance, ID, or even post-mortem photography, but rather from the personal and family contexts of each victim. These are images taken from larger photographs that in the hours following the killings were no doubt hastily gathered by relatives from mantelpieces, presses, purses and family albums. In almost every case the individual has clearly been cropped out of a larger picture that captured, in addition to the victim, his family and friends. Although it is unlikely that this effect was apparent, let alone of particular concern, to readers of newspapers in those early days of February 1972, the severe cropping of the images serves to reinforce the effect of an abrupt separation from an original and pleasurable prior context. The original photograph of Jackie Duddy, for example, showed him posing with a group of young boxers at the Long Tower Boy's Club: he wears a string vest and dons a pair of huge boxing gloves with which he half protects his face. The photographs of Hugh Gilmore, John Young and Kevin McElhinney were taken in photobooths (probably in Woolworth's on Ferryquay Street or Wellworth's in Waterloo Place). The images of Gerald McKinney and William McKinney could also have been taken in a photobooth, but both have a particular quality that suggests they may have been taken in a professional photographer's studio. William Nash is playing a guitar outside his house in Dunree Gardens in the Creggan. Jim Wray is standing arm-in-arm with a young woman. Michael Kelly wears a long white jacket in a photograph taken by a colleague during their lunch break. Michael McDaid squints into the sun as he crouches down to hold a baby. Bernard McGuigan sits with his wife in a nightclub, both of them smiling broadly at the photographer. And, perhaps most poignantly, Gerald Donaghy, as a child of eight or nine years of age, seems to stare into space in a photograph taken to mark his First Holy Communion.

So there is a tension at work here. From the moment these individual images appear in the newspaper grid, they take on a new kind of existence. Transformed through the 'accident' of death and through the media's need to show them in relation to an event, they are forced to co-exist. Thirteen men and boys – most of whom did not know each other – now dwell together in death in a sort of spectral convocation. These animated, mostly smiling faces become the Bloody Sunday dead, fated always, at least as far as the print media are concerned, to be placed in a rigid arrangement of images alongside, above and below their fellow victims. But this formal visual uniformity is rendered unstable by the fact that the images insist upon a quite different register of meaning to that suggested by the arrangement of their 'portrait' images in newspaper media. As we look at the gridlocked faces of the Bloody Sunday dead we realise that we are actually in the presence of separate and entirely unique faces as they look out at us and address us with the gaze that they once held for a fraction of a second during a summer afternoon on a beach in Donegal, or a lunch break from work, or an evening out on the town – times and places that have nothing whatever to do with Bloody Sunday itself.

Following the publication of Lord Widgery's report on 18 April 1972, the photographic grid reappeared in some newspapers or appeared for the first time in others. The *Belfast Telegraph* (the north-west edition of which sold thousands of copies every evening in Derry) did not use the portraits in its coverage of the shootings themselves, but it did feature them to accompany its generally favourable reporting of Widgery's findings. The dead appeared on page 12 of the 20 April edition, under the headline 'Sniper Fired First, No Breakdown in Army Discipline but some Soldiers Fired Recklessly. What happened on Bloody Sunday'. So here the portraits were anchored by the interpretative framework of Widgery: not 'What Happened on Bloody Sunday?' but 'What Happened on Bloody Sunday'. Accompanying each photograph were one or two eyewitness accounts to the tribunal, but each entry concluded with Widgery's brief rulings on the circumstances of each man's death. Most other British newspapers followed the same pattern. For those newspapers that carried the portrait photographs, the grid now suggested not so much the men's guilt (not even those most sympathetic to the British case could conjure conclusive guilt out of Widgery's findings) but certainly their complicity in their own deaths. This was not quite a collection of mugshots, but it was to all intents and purposes an assemblage of the criminally complicit. In official terms the event was closed and the brief media life of the portraits all but disappeared as, in the wider context, the coverage of the region settled into a regular pattern of violent acts followed by moral denunciation, 'the politics of the last atrocity', as Gerry Adams once put it. But in Derry – beginning with the first anniversary – the portraits of the dead men (now with the addition of John Johnston, who died in July

1972 from medical complications following the injuries he received on the day of the march) began to take on a new function. Now they appeared as the ghost reappears, as a troubling presence, as a reminder of times out-of-joint, as a demand for redress.

Mobilising the dead

In the wake of the theorisations of the photographic image undertaken by Roland Barthes, Philippe Dubois, Susan Sontag and others, it has become something of a truism to say that photography and death share certain affinities. Dubois deploys the term 'thanatography' to describe the photograph's deathly silence,[5] while Barthes describes the experience of viewing the photograph as a form of 'flat death'.[6] However, what we want to stress in the following analysis is not so much the absoluteness associated with death, nor perhaps comforting belief that the photographic image may retain elements of what Sontag describes as the 'real'.[7] Instead, we want to discuss the photographs as having something to do with the unfinishedness of spectrality. It is photography *and* spectrality, photography *as* spectrality, that is key to understanding the function of the images of the dead in the campaigns that have led from Bloody Sunday to the Saville Inquiry.

From the first anniversary of the killings the images of the fourteen dead men began a more public life as they were carried by families in the 'Ceremony of the Innocents', a procession of some 15,000 people who, after attending an interdenominational requiem mass at St Mary's Chapel in the Creggan, followed the route of the original protest but this time aiming not for the Guildhall in the city's centre but for Rossville Street, where most of the killings took place. Just outside the Rossville Flats, Lord Fenner Brockway (who was present at the march the previous year) cut the first sod of earth at the site of the proposed Bloody Sunday memorial, an obelisk that would be unveiled the following year. What is striking about this and other early commemorative parades is the way in which the photographic images of the dead men were held aloft at the head of the procession in much the same way as icons of saints are held in Catholic pilgrimages. In fact, the other commemorative marches in the 1970s followed rather rigidly the protocols of Catholic funeral processions, in which it is the male relatives and friends who lead the way, with the women and children following. On the first anniversary march, those carrying the small placards featuring black-and-white reproductions of the portraits were predominantly adult males. Eamon Melaugh's memorable images of the placards held by relatives of the dead show a somewhat makeshift arrangement: an unadorned platform featuring people bearing blown-up versions of the photographs that had appeared so widely the previous year. And perhaps through an accident of design, the faces of the dead obscure the heads and faces of the people holding the placards. Situated in the very place in which the killings took place, the photographs produce an effect of 'homogeneous empty time'.[8] Here, in the very heart of the killing ground, is an uncanny reminder of what had happened a year earlier. But this is far more than simple commemoration, because the photographs, juxtaposed with civil rights banners and the speeches made from the platform, were also an enjoinder to justice: justice for those who were still interned without trial. Poignantly, uncannily, this was exactly the same demand made by the crowd who had attempted to assemble peacefully twelve months earlier.

No longer constrained to mass cards or to the pages of newspapers, these images of the dead men now began to move in and around the public sphere. They formed a continuation of the protest of the previous year, while adding a supplement that strengthened the protest itself. The shift from private to public brought about by the displaying of the photographs (or manipulations of them) changed the emphasis from one of emotional reminder to that of ethical and political demand. The images were carried not as part of a firmly established ceremony but as part of a dynamic campaign that was, initially, a continuation of the anti-internment protests but then, from 1992, became much more concerned with the need for a new and independent inquiry into the killings themselves. Throughout the long history of the Bloody Sunday

Figure 2. First Bloody Sunday commemoration: platform party holding placards
(*Photo courtesy Eamon Melaugh*)

commemorations, the photographic images have been actively deployed each time. Carried at the head of the march, held aloft at the very spot in which the killings occurred, they function as an enjoinder to look, to contemplate, to act. They are a forceful return of the repressed in a fleeting and uncanny moment of spectrality.

This is a phenomenon both powerful and banal: every photograph, Barthes asserts, is spectral in that we look at an image of someone who is always caught for a moment in the past and, to that extent, is dead and gone, and yet here they are in front of us, in our hands, looking out to us. The gaze of those who have gone, of the dead, cannot fail to produce effects in the here and now. Although the image does not speak, 'it does not', as Jacques Derrida said about the ghost, 'do nothing'.[9] All photographs produce these effects, but when those photographs are made part of an ethical/ political campaign that attempts to draw attention to the injustice of the deaths to which those images bear witness, then the aura of spectrality is made more potent. The photographs of the dead men serve as a memorial, a memory trace of loved ones now distant and gone. But they also function in the public sphere as an apostrophic demand: 'Do not forget what happened to us cruelly, unjustly on that day.' Key to the ways in which these images have been translated and mobilised by the groups campaigning on the families' behalf is a refusal to allow silence to settle on the individual pictures, which also serve metonymically for the community of Derry and beyond that for the nationalists of Northern Ireland. Bloody Sunday was an attempt by the British state to silence a recently politicised population and in the short term it worked. Scores of contemporary accounts reflect the state of stunned silence that fell on the city of Derry in the days after the killings and this quality is addressed both in film and poetry, discussed in later chapters. Lord Widgery's inquiry sought to impose another form of official silence on the event and took only fourteen witness statements into account, leaving over 450 outside the parameters of the inquiry, whilst almost all military accounts were included.[10]

However, over the course of the next thirty years and more there was a refusal by the families and their supporters to allow the official forgetting in the wake of Widgery to go uncontested. Taking their place at the centre of this process the portraits now became the manifestation of the wound, the open cut that disturbed the surface of official discourse. These mobilisations of the portrait images worked with, and in some ways against, more official markers of Bloody Sunday, such as the limestone memorial on Rossville Street, or even the minor-monumental mural of the dead produced by the Bogside Artists. The photographs of the faces of the dead are far more resistant to the monument's singularisation of the experience of the event: as Barthes has argued, photography has 'renounced the monument'.[11] For the reasons we set out earlier regarding the differences insisted upon by the various settings and *mises en scène* of each photographic image, the portraits of the fourteen dead men refuse to allow the event to become settled or abstracted in the ways suggested by monuments, plaques or murals.

Faces in the crowd

We have referred several times to the focus on faces in these images. We do this quite deliberately: it is in the presentation of the faces of the dead men that resides the power of the collective layout as a direct response to the effacing of identity undertaken by the British Army and subsequent British administrations. On the day of the march the British authorities set out to confront, in their terms, a faceless crowd, an indiscriminate mass of Derry young hooligans/yobbos/terrorists/organisers of, and participants in, a march that challenged the authority of the state to intern members of the nationalist community without trial and to contain a community within its defined boundary. On that day all of those marching, regardless of their political affiliations, motivations and reservations, were simply a 'crowd', an assemblage that Zygmunt Bauman defines as having to do precisely with the 'loss of face':

> The urban crowd is not a collection of individuals. It is rather an indiscriminate, formless aggregate in which individuality dissolves. The crowd is faceless, but so are its units. Units are replaceable and disposable. Neither their entry nor their disappearance makes a difference. It is through their facelessness that the mobile units of urban congestion are defused as the possible sources of social engagement.[12]

When we realise that the NICRA march from the Creggan to the Guildhall was, in fact, an 'illegal' protest, then the crowd itself becomes criminalised: all those who participated in it were, by definition, criminals. Witness the response to the massacre in the *Daily Mail* editorial of Monday 31 January. Under the headline 'Who are the real killers?' the leader writer opined, 'British bullets will be found in most of their bodies . . . but the blood is on the consciences of irresponsible political leaders and the fanatical IRA . . . Those who died were not martyrs to Civil Rights (though already last night they were being promoted as such). They were terrorists, or fodder for terrorists. They died that anti-British propaganra [*sic*] might flourish.' It is not at all surprising, therefore, that the concentration upon the faces of the victims of Bloody Sunday has been so key to all subsequent commemorations and campaigns. Indeed, the presentation of faces as synecdoche for entire communities' fears, successes and aspirations is a striking element of Northern Irish political imagery. At the unveiling of a mural to commemorate the death of his son and a fellow republican at the hands of the British Army in August 1973, Patrick Mulvenna, a member of the

Ballymurphy Mural Project Committee, articulated the need to present the faces of those killed:

> We wanted this tribute to portray our dead in a human way. For too long the British and our political enemies portrayed republicans as 'faceless gunmen' in their attempts to criminalise the struggle, so we decided that we would present our dead as real human beings.[13]

We find echoes of Bloody Sunday commemorations in this father's desire to put a human face on a combatant who, in official discourse, will never be anything other than 'gun-man' or 'man-of-violence'. One can also look at work by the artist Willie Doherty, such as *Same Difference* (1990) and *They're All the Same* (1991), which take as their subjects the disjuncture between, on the one hand, media portraits of, respectively, Donna Maguire and Nessan Quinlivan and, on the other, narratives and words that challenge the simple notions of terrorist or murderer.

There is a historical dimension to this desire to insist that the protesting crowd is never simply a faceless mass but is in fact constituted of many human subjects with various degrees of commitment and various types of reservation concerning the issues that have mobilised the crowd of which they find themselves a part. For example, confronting Edmund Burke's description of the insurrectionary crowds in *Reflections on the Revolution in France* (1790) as the 'swinish multitude' and Hippolyte Taine's later depiction of the same crowds as made up of the 'dregs of society', 'bandits', 'thieves', 'savages', 'beggars', 'prostitutes', the social historian George Rudé sought to identify, in Asa Briggs's phrase, 'the faces in the crowd'.[14] By attending to the multiple nature of these faces and their associated identities Rudé strove to distinguish the complexity of 'social and political interests, grievances, ideas, and aspirations' at work in any given protest.[15] The implications of Rudé's groundbreaking work, on crowds in sixteenth- and seventeenth-century European political protest, for Bloody Sunday commemorations are clear. For over thirty years there has been a refusal by the families and their supporters to allow the language of the British state to define both the terms of the event and those who 'experienced' it. From the first anniversary through to the most recent, the photographic portraits of the dead have been at the centre (that is, near the front) of the march from the Creggan to the Bloody Sunday memorial in the Bogside. Accompanying the Irish tricolour, anti-internment banners and crosses bearing the names of the dead, there have always been placards or banners displaying their faces.

It is somewhat surprising that it was not until 1992 that the first mural depicting the dead of Bloody Sunday appeared in Derry. Produced under the auspices of the Bloody Sunday Initiative (BSI), the image of the fourteen men occupied a gable wall at the lower end of Westland Street, just metres from where several of them had been killed on the rubble barricade. The belatedness of this image may be accounted for by several factors. First, that from 1974 there had been a permanent physical reminder of the dead of Bloody Sunday in the shape of the 'official' NICRA-sponsored limestone monument at Joseph Place. Second, that images of the dead men's faces were displayed annually on small placards during the commorative marches, as well as in the *In Memoriam* pages of the *Derry Journal*. Third, and related to the above, that images of Bloody Sunday itself were renewed annually by the publicity posters produced initially by NICRA and then followed by the various groups that organised or contributed towards the annual commemorative events (Sinn Féin, NICRA/Derry Civil Rights Association, the Bloody Sunday Organizing Committee, Derry Frontline, the Bloody Sunday Initiative, and the Bloody Sunday Justice Campaign).[16]

Facing Free Derry Wall and across the road from the memorial stone, this first mural to the Bloody Sunday victims was at the time of its production a startling affair. Unconnected to any political grouping and displaying no message other than 'The Day Innocence Died', a montage of faces familiar from the media coverage of the killings was painted onto what was increasingly the favoured surface for Derry muralists: the gable-end of Northern Ireland Housing Executive maisonettes. However, unlike the stark black-and-white images of twenty years earlier, this mural presented the faces of the men in vibrant colours – blue, green, red, white and yellow. Furthermore, not all of the images had been widely seen before: for example, the image of Paddy Docherty was cropped from his wedding photograph, and the image of Hugh Gilmore was adapted from a hitherto unpublished photobooth shot.

In his perceptive discussion of the cultural geography of the Bogside, Graham Dawson argues that the murals that constitute, in the Bogside Artists' phrase, 'The People's Gallery',

> install at the heart of the location vivid images of the past that took place here, creating a kind of living-art installation that weaves memory into the scene of everyday life . . . Through the selection and presentation of their imagery, the murals are a visible manifestation of the political counter-memory of injustice and resistance, whilst in their location they also contribute to the cultural and psychic function of the memorial space as a whole, in its symbolic reclaiming and 'detoxifying' of the site or the atrocity – a contaminated space of trauma and death – by and for the local community.[17]

In line with the Bogside Artists' interest in marking particularly resonant anniversaries with new paintings and displays, the 25th anniversary saw two new developments. The first was a new mural depicting the events of Bloody Sunday. Measuring six metres by eight metres, the mural is a condensation of four distinct moments, captured by media images, of 30 January 1972: (1) the parade as it comes down

William Street towards Barrier 14, (2) the organisers of the protest aboard Thomas McGlinchey's flat-bedded coal lorry, (3) the Civil Rights Association banner covered with Barney McGuigan's blood, and (4) the unforgettable moment caught on BBC and CBS television at the junction of Chamberlain Street and Waterloo Street when a British soldier attempts to halt a group of men attempting to carry the dying Jackie Duddy to safety.

There are several striking aspects to the image. There is, first of all, a tremendously clear delineation of faces, whether they are the faces of

Figure 3. Bloody Sunday mural, Bogside, Derry. By The Bogside Artists
(*Photo courtesy Tom Herron*)

those occupying the foreground of the image (the men carrying and assisting Duddy), the mid-ground (the organisers on the lorry), or the background (the marchers). There is, of course, one exception to this emphasis on facial delineation and that is the soldier, who, in occupying the extreme foreground, is presented in profile with his face concealed by a gas mask. Finger on the trigger of his SLR and instantly recognisable by his insignia and helmet as a member of the Paratroop Regiment, the soldier seems in a somewhat uncertain relationship to the events narrated by the image. Whilst he stands on the blood-soaked civil rights banner and whilst he poses a clear threat, at the same time there is the suggestion that he is an onlooker to the drama unfolding as a result of his and his colleagues' actions. Almost every face in the mural is witness to this terrible scene and, when we factor in the point of view of the person looking up at the mural, the soldier is suddenly caught in a matrix of gazes. Although he remains anonymous and dangerous, his actions are seen by the multiple eyewitnesses to the event. This effect is accentuated in the Bogside Artists' revision of the mural, in that faces that initially looked away from the soldier now turn their gaze fully towards him.

The Bloody Sunday mural has, at its very centre, one of the most memorable icons of the entire day: Father Daly's white handkerchief. Much has been written and said about this and other white handkerchiefs held aloft as people ventured out to aid those killed or injured by the soldiers,[18] so it is no huge surprise that an image produced to commemorate Bloody Sunday should have incorporated this item; an item that Graham Dawson has described as playing a key part in the creation and maintenance of the 'post-memory' of Bloody Sunday. Signifying a range of associations – fragility, purity, intimacy, surrender, ceasefire – and put to a number of uses on the afternoon of 30 January 1972 – as masks to avoid identification and to provide meagre protection against CS gas, as makeshift bandages for wounds, as small flags to indicate that help was being offered to an injured person – the handkerchief in this mural is virtually contiguous with Jackie Duddy's face and exposed abdomen. As he ventured up Chamberlain Street shouting 'Hold Your Fire', Edward Daly's hankie was in fact covered in Duddy's blood. He held it in his right hand, while in his left he carried a dark-coloured scarf or jacket. In the mural the hankie is unblemished, presumably to maintain the black-and-white colour coding of the image, and so as not to detract from the splash of colour at the foot of the image where the civil rights banner used to cover the dead body of Bernard McGuigan is being trampled on by the soldier. The image has a strong vectorialism: everything seems to flow down towards the lower foreground of the image where the banner-cum-shroud is placed. In the earlier version of the mural, this banner was thoroughly besmattered with blood, to the extent that its legend, 'Civil Rights', was entirely overlaid by the colour red, in the shape of the cross of St George, which forms the basis, of course, of the Ulster (Six Counties) flag. In the revised version, the extent of blood-signifying colour is more limited and the cruciform has disappeared. Now the legend is not so much occluded by red paint as by the growth of shrubs alongside the railings that run beneath the mural.

In producing their People's Gallery, the Bogside Artists have clearly gone to great lengths to create an inclusive and dynamic narrative of events and processes that have shaped the political and cultural fabric of the Bogside. Their work does not, to be sure, create a monolithic version of the area and its inhabitants' recent history, but there are elements within even the most apparently benign and ameliorative images that suggest a certain violence of representation.

In choosing to commemorate Bloody Sunday, the Bogside Artists were perforce obliged to isolate certain elements and moments from the array of available images of that afternoon. But in selecting from the image bank of that afternoon, the Artists unavoidably introduce framing devices that, whilst paying homage to well-established figures and images of Bloody Sunday, actually work to reduce the simultaneously collective and individual acts of heroism performed under the most severe of conditions. In its depiction of the party assisting Jackie Duddy the mural has three men carrying the body: Charles Glenn, William Barber and Liam Bradley. But this rendering of the scene does not accord with the evidence as caught by BBC and CBS television film crews, nor is it consistent with Fred Hoare's photograph, nor with the images taken by Fulvio Grimaldi: all of which capture images in which Duddy's body is carried, not by three, but by four men – Glenn, Barber, Bradley, and William McCrystal. It was McCrystal who told the soldier (and the other soldiers beyond him) to 'get away'. In addition to this immediate group and Father Daly were several men and women who accompanied the party up Chamberlain Street towards the soldiers.

There is no suggestion here that anyone is being airbrushed out of history, but what the elision reveals is the difficulty of achieving a form of representation that effects an adequate balance between artistic freedom and ethical responsibility, between the dicates of aesthetics and the demands of community-embedded project such as the Bogside Artists that has as one of its aims 'to tell the story of the Bogside'. The elision and the concentration on established icons within the Bloody Sunday mural reiterates a story that must be insisted upon until its veridicity is *once and for all* established, but at the same time it runs the risk of producing an alternative authoritative truth that is just as rigid (although, of course, without the deleterious effects) as the 'official truth' against which it sets itself up in an ethics of remembrance and narration. Such an ethically-driven and community-embedded practice should not itself be immune to critique when its own production

Figure 4. Free Derry Corner, Bogside, Derry *(Photo courtesy John Lynch)*

unnecessarily limits the possible number of interpretations of an event the multiple truths of which require the fullest and most honest recognition.

The second significant development was the construction of large-scale images of the victims. Over the years of commemoration the images of the dead men's faces varied in size and coloration, but they retained their essential characteristics: small-scale images carried by individuals either at the head of the march or behind the crosses bearing the names of the dead. However, for this 25th anniversary they appeared dramatically enlarged in a series of hand-painted images produced over a three-night period in a community hall in the Creggan by the Bogside Artists. These images, each one now held aloft by two people, took their part in an increasingly professional visualisation of commemoration.

By displaying these banners and guiding them through the commemorating crowd, and then moving them to strategic points around the Bogside and the City Walls overlooking the area, those wielding them carried out a manoeuvre with several distinct effects. Most immediately and most simply, the banners provided a focus for the commemoration (thereby strengthening the cohesion of the crowd), while at the same time (by placing so much emphasis on the faces of the dead) they disaggregated the notion of the crowd as a faceless mass. The banners also linked the present-day commemoration not only to the civil rights march on 30 January 1972 but also to each subsequent commemoration: this is a version of Elias Canetti's 'double crowd' – the sense of two (or many) crowds composed of both the living and the dead operating synchronically.[19]

Of all the anniversaries, this would prove to be the most decisive in the campaign to establish a proper inquiry into the killings. In addition to the requiem mass at St Mary's, the march from the Creggan to the Bogside and the observances at the Rossville memorial, the commemorative events included the launch of Don Mullan's groundbreaking book *Eyewitness Bloody Sunday*, as well as addresses at public meetings by leading academic and political figures in the campaign for an independent inquiry, including Tim Pat Coogan, Seamus Deane, Eamonn McCann and Martin McGuinness. To coincide with the weekend, the government of Ireland announced that it had commissioned its own report into the new evidence that had emerged in the preceding months: this report would appear in June of 1997. The Pat Finucane Centre, under whose auspices the commemorative events were now organised, managed to galvanise huge public interest in these events. Their efforts were aided by a *Derry Journal* special 25th anniversary supplement and by the cultural events in the Bogside organised by *Féile '97*.[20] By far the most important development of the weekend was the launch on the morning of Thursday 30 January of the Bloody Sunday Trust, the families' campaigning group that would steer all subsequent commemorations and campaigns. One of the most

Figure 5. Twenty-fifth anniversary commemoration, Free Derry Wall, Bogside, Derry *(Photo courtesy PA Photos)*

notable features of these particular commemorations was a poem written by two young people from Derry. Killian Mullan and Sharon Meenan's 'I Wasn't Even Born' was featured both in the *Derry Journal* supplement and in the Pat Finucane Centre's publicity leaflet for the weekend's events. Deployed alongside the banners, the poem provided one of the most dramatic moments of all Bloody Sunday commemorations.

As the dead men were named in the poem, the Bogside Artists' banners with shimmering images of their faces were raised on the hill overlooking Free Derry Corner. Will Kelly of the Bogside Artists relates how 'the idea of hoisting the banners in sequence in sync with the poem was our idea. Whose exactly? Nobody knows; but we all recollect it ensued from a prior discussion we had about infusing some "performance art" into the proceedings. Our hope was to give the genre some appropriate gravitas and maybe add something to the art form.'[21] The undeniable drama of this moment is a product of intersecting strands of commemoration (the appearance of the fresh images, the mnemonic and evocative power of the poem itself, the innovative and ironic use of the spaces of the Bogside itself), brilliantly orchestrated to produce a moment of commemorative intensity. Following the 25th anniversary, the faces of the dead were no longer confined to the route of the march from the Creggan to the Bogside. Increasingly they appeared elsewhere: on the Walls of Derry, for example, to highlight the speculation that snipers of the Royal Anglian Regiment had contributed to the carnage of Bloody Sunday and, in January 2003, in Whitehall, opposite the gates of Downing Street, as part of the families' campaign to have official British Army photographic evidence released to the inquiry.

The use of the portraits of the Bloody Sunday victims by campaigners for a new inquiry represented a dramatic innovation in the poetics of Northern Irish parades and commemorations – 'performances of memory', as Neil Jarman has described them. Most parades function as attempts to sustain, through strictly regulated acts of repetition, a particular version of history. They are, especially in the loyalist tradition, assertions of the sameness of past, present and future. Their success depends on obsessively choreographed acts of mimesis. Jarman's memorable description of the Orange Order's annual Glorious Twelfth parades explains:

> For that day the Orangemen constitute themselves as a replica army, and their parade mimics the departure to, and return from, war . . . As the contemporary community relives the events of the past they become contemporary events: the performance is no longer restricted to a symbolic meaning, the enactment has real effects in real time . . . For the performance to be disrupted or cancelled would be to transform history, to rupture the simultaneity of past and present and make the future uncertain.[22]

The similarities between this type of performance and the Bloody Sunday commemorations are outweighed by their differences. The Orange parades are backward-looking celebrations of victory, all the more hysterical because they promote the preservation and continuation of an increasingly threatened supremacy. The annual processions in Derry also refer to a past event, but only in order to move forward to a future moment when that event will be recognised for what it was. The flow of the crowd in and around the changed spaces of the Creggan, the Brandywell and the Bogside is not a march along a 'traditional' route deriving from the dominance of space by triumphalist ritual. The procession begins at the Creggan shops and makes its way via Rathlin Drive, Southway, the Lone Moor Road, Brandywell Road, the Lecky Road, Westland Street, Marlborough Terrace, William Street and Rossville Street to the Bloody Sunday memorial at Joseph Place. The marches – in which the banner-portraits play a key part – describe the pathways and the fissures of a continuously changing political and geographic landscape. The monumentality of the Bloody Sunday commemorations is a minor monumentality that is never a repetition of a mythical point of origin for an imaginary identity but that is constitutive of a demand for an open future distinguished by justice and truth. Paul Ricoeur describes this as partly one of obligation: 'The duty, therefore, is one which concerns the future; it is an imperative directed towards the future, which is exactly the opposite side of the traumatic character of the humiliations and wounds of history'.[23] There is an undoubted quality of mourning at work here but not one of melancholia, which is characterised by Freud as one of despair. On the annual processions the portraits of the fourteen dead men function not as an attempt to halt the flow of time but rather to draw attention to the untimeliness of their deaths, and to draw the commemorations' participants and observers towards the future, towards tangible and definable outcomes.

From Derry to Downing Street and beyond, the images have come a long way since they were gathered by staff of the *Derry Journal* in the hours following the naming of the dead on the evening of 30 January 1972. Since then they have been reproduced on mass cards, obituary notices, commemorative posters, newspaper front pages, gable-end murals, small placards and then large-scale banners carried on the annual commemorations. They have appeared in books and in television documentaries. In the past few years they have formed a key part of the 'Hidden Truths' exhibition that, following its opening on 29 January 2000 at the UCR/California Museum of Photography, toured major cities in the USA. They occur regularly on websites relating to the Northern Irish conflict. At press conferences hosted by and on behalf of the families, images of the dead are always present. For the 35th anniversary parade they were returned to the march itself, by being posted at strategic sites along the route; but now it was not their faces that looked out at the passing marches, but images of the men pho- tographed with their families and friends. And when Lord Saville finally produces his report they will, no doubt, reappear in the newspaper and television media, to be subjected to yet more manipulations and inter- pretations. Perhaps then they will be able to cease their annual journeys through the streets of Derry and, as with all ghosts, when the wrong- doing to which they bear testimony is finally recognised, find peace.

3

Virtual Justice

Saville and the
Technologies of Truth

The 'perfect crime' does not consist in killing the victim or the witnesses (that adds new crimes to the first one and aggravates the difficulty of effacing everything), but rather in obtaining the silence of the witnesses, the deafness of the judges, and the inconsistency (insanity) of the testimony.[1]

Introduction

Bloody Sunday came back into the consciousness of the general public with the announcement by Prime Minister Tony Blair of a new inquiry on 29 January 1998. There had been an inquiry into Bloody Sunday in 1972 under the chairmanship of the Lord Chief Justice, Lord Widgery. Lord Widgery had come to the conclusion that some of those killed had indeed handled weapons or been close to individuals firing them and that, in general, the soldiers had behaved in accordance with their standing orders. According to him, the blame for the deaths lay with the organisers of the march:

> There would have been no deaths in Londonderry on 30 January if those who organised the illegal march had not thereby created a highly dangerous situation in which a clash between the demonstrators and the security forces was almost inevitable.[2]

This official judgment by the highest judge in England generated profound and lasting bitterness in Derry and amongst the nationalist population of Northern Ireland. It stands as an enduring example of the distorted and fundamentally biased nature of the British law and justice system as it applies to the Northern Ireland conflict. Seamus Dunn comments: 'By any standards the Report is an evasive and complacent work, full of unquestioned certainties and veiled in the niceties and subterfuges of legal language'.[3] A substantial and detailed analysis of the shortcomings of the report and the processes of Widgery's inquiry can be found in Dermot Walsh's book *Bloody Sunday and the Rule of Law in Northern Ireland*. In this he writes:

Twenty-seven years later it would be perverse even to suggest that the tribunal was successful in fulfilling its official mandate. The very fact that an unprecedented second tribunal of inquiry had to be appointed to investigate the very same matters is in itself powerful testimony of the failure of the Widgery Tribunal.[4]

In a wider sense, the new inquiry under Mark Saville was not simply a staging of an inquiry to determine a truth but a political intervention to help stabilise the ongoing problematic of a peace process. It is a strategic construct that seeks to establish the past in the present in a period of transition away from violent conflict. In his statement to the House of Commons outlining its function, Tony Blair concluded:

> I believe that it is in everyone's interest that the truth be established and told. That is also the way forward to the necessary reconciliation that will be such an important part of building a secure future for the people of Northern Ireland. I ask Hon. Members of all parties to support our proposal for this inquiry.[5]

Reconciliation through truth and the moving towards a shared future, therefore, would seem to be its motivation. Certainly the travesty of justice that was the Widgery Report was an obstacle to peace that needed to be overcome. What the new inquiry pointed to was the recognition of a profound injustice, but one which, of course, had operated through the formalised procedures of the judicial system and its functionaries, who are well versed in the obfuscatory tactics of legal procedure, and which could make the emergence of clear and unambiguous truths seem, at times, very distant. At the heart of this legal process is a fundamental crisis of truth that the judges must seek to resolve through hearing witness testimony and examining visual material and all other elements of supporting evidence.

 The demand for justice is, in this context then, a challenge to the law of the British state manifested in Lord Widgery's Report. Indeed, when Bernadette McAliskey, who, as Bernadette Devlin, had been one of the platform speakers on Bloody Sunday, was called to give testimony to the Saville inquiry, she stated that 'this should be somewhere else where the accused is not running the party'.[6] Such a statement raises the question of whether justice can be achieved within the same legal framework as that which engendered the act of injustice in the first place. In a substantial analysis of Bloody Sunday and the issues of law, Angela Hegarty addresses this paradox: 'the question remains whether law is capable of providing that accountability and arriving at some form of truth'.[7] It may just be the case that the framework itself is now different. It is barely conceivable that British Prime Minister Tony Blair would have anything approaching the influence on Mark Saville as that exercised by Prime Minister Heath when he 'reminded' Lord Widgery 'that we are in Northern Ireland fighting not only a military war but a propaganda

war'. Can the paradox of a system of law contradicting its own prece-
dent and denying its own history then claim to legitimately pass
judgment on the events described? It might be apposite to remember
what Walter Benjamin had to say about any such institutional discourse:
'There is no document of civilization which is not at the same time a
document of barbarism.'[8] The demand for justice, therefore, is made by
individuals engaged in a struggle for recognition and a particular kind of
remembering. Injustice is always a singularity, a historically specific act
that brings forth the ghost (the demand for redress) and the question is:
can it ever be laid to rest?

Memory

> Memory, both personal and collective, is essential for the work of
> justice, and therefore ghosts, as the intermediaries between the dead
> and the living, are key figures of justice, the heralds, if you will, of a
> justice that can never present itself.[9]

One of the most significant aspects of the new inquiry under Lord
Saville was the level of technology mobilised to display, mediate and disseminate the proceedings. Clearly one reason for this was the very real
need to be 'seen' to be acting fairly and objectively to overcome the
deep-rooted cynicism towards the machinery of justice in the province
amongst the Catholics of Derry and the North of Ireland. The British
government was well aware of the need to satisfy the high level of
scrutiny the inquiry would be under. Whilst not actually televised at any
point, the visibility of the display screens, computer monitors, virtual
reality software and online viewable witness testimony raised the
inquiry to a particular kind of drama, a staging with a very clear sense
of an audience in mind. But why was there such a high level of technological support for what was essentially a judicial investigation
(importantly, one which was intended to be inquisitorial and not adversarial in nature) that would seek to establish the truth of the events
leading up to and including the events of 30 January 1972? A key issue
is the question of the individual memories of an event thirty years in the
past of a group of people who had subsequently adopted a wide range of
coping strategies in relation to what they had experienced. Coupled with
this was a geographical space that was much changed from how it had
been in 1972. Arguably, therefore, in different ways, this scale of technological support was needed to overcome the temporal and
geographical 'gap' between the different experiential elements. Functioning, apparently, as a necessary supplement, it actually plays, as
Jacques Derrida observes of such a concept, a rather more active role.[10]
We can see that there is, actually, always a technology at work with any
system of law. Within the new Bloody Sunday inquiry technology was
used variously to record, to amplify, to disseminate, to confirm, to

remind and to make visible that which is presumed to be primary: the speaking subject. But without the technology could it be said that there even was an inquiry?

Memory was necessarily at the heart of the process of establishing what counsel for the inquiry Christopher Clarke, QC, defined in the opening speech as the fundamental aim of the new proceedings: to establish 'the truth, pure and simple' of what happened on Bloody Sunday. In the dramatic adaptation of the inquiry there is a scene of a witness being questioned by a QC for the military as to whether they have or have not watched any films about Bloody Sunday or read any of the books on the subject: the premise being, presumably, that any testimony asserting a memory of the events could have been contaminated by subsequent representations. Given the repeated defence of many soldiers involved in the shooting that day that they were unable to remember important details (one was reported to have replied 84 times that he could not recall any events of the day)[11], the question of the reliability of witness memory was important. Crucially, then, the question of witness memory of Bloody Sunday raises difficult issues about experience, sense and narrative. Patrick Hayes and Jim Campbell in their book on the psychological trauma suffered by the families of those killed and injured on Bloody Sunday point to the nature of what processes of memory formation can be seen to be at work:

> Unassimilated traumatic experiences are stored in what Horowitz (1997) refers to as 'active memory', accounting for the cycles of denial and intrusions with nightmares, flashbacks and the need to re-enact trauma. This process continues until the person develops a new mental schema, either positive or negative, to explain what has happened.[12]

As they point out, for some of those who witnessed actual fatal shootings what was most troubling were the gaps in their memory and unaccounted-for time periods when they know they must have been doing something but just could not remember: 'In an otherwise logical and detailed account [the witness] could not recall details of experiences that spanned a ten-minute period, from the scene of the shooting until he arrived home.'[13] Similarly, Don Mullan recounts that, as the Paras attacked, 'I escaped through Glenfada Park but there are several minutes of that afternoon of which I have absolutely no memory'.[14]

Not surprisingly, accounts of the day by witnesses and participants on the march describe the chaos that ensued as soldiers started opening fire. It seems that the nature of the event itself means that it defies simple understanding that can be communicated as an absolute truth. Given what was perceived as hostile questioning by solicitors for the soldiers and the doubts then cast on witness testimony (typifying the fundamentally uneven nature of any legal exchange), the issue of confusion or contradiction would seem significant. Yet, again, it points to the nature of memory of something such as Bloody Sunday as, by definition, tending towards the confused. Cathy Caruth writes of this experience and the relationship between the individual psyche and reality:

> In its general definition, trauma is described as the response to an unexpected or overwhelming violent event or events that are not fully grasped as they occur, but return later in repeated flashbacks, nightmares, and other repetitive phenomena. Traumatic experience, beyond the psychological dimension of suffering it involves, suggests a certain paradox: that the most direct seeing of a violent event may occur as an absolute inability to know it; that immediacy, paradoxically, may take the form of belatedness.[15]

It would be useful, therefore, to establish some understanding of the relationship between the individual memory of an event and the collective social realm within which it would be formed. It must be emphasised that this is not to raise doubts about the veracity of individual testimony of the witnesses to what happened. There is a very clear distinction between a suspicion of systematic and organised revision of statements and testimony, as Dermot Walsh indicates in relation to soldiers' evidence to the Widgery tribunal, and a wider sense of the social process by which individuals seek to make sense of that which they witnessed.

Given the nature of the judicial process at work in the inquiry it would seem pertinent to consider aspects of the different processes at work. What is presupposed is the ability to re-present a moment of self-presence located temporally in the past. In one sense, such a formulation goes to the question of subjectivity, where the seemingly unified and coherent subject, rather than being defined as a transcendent subject merely recollecting a memory, is actually cohered by memory as a process of stabilisation. It seems evident that one of the problems of the Saville inquiry was the, sometimes, glaring gap between contemporaneous accounts of witnesses being replayed nearly thirty years later as though somehow the intervening years become merely transparent. Again, this is not to somehow suggest that any testimony is therefore to be considered with suspicion or cynicism – the answer to the question 'Did you hear or see gunmen firing at the soldiers?' can be presumed to be consistent in general terms – but we should consider the relationship between the chaotic, traumatic and fragmentary burst of short-term memory of parts of that day all those years before and the more organised structure of long-term memory. Deleuze and Guattari distinguish between these formations as characterised by, on the one hand, rhizomatic and, on the other, arboreal structures. The former is short-term memory not yet classified or sorted, the latter is that which has become translated into a centralised matrix of the fixed and self-evident.[16] Like any such distinction, the terms are not absolute but, rather, usefully illustrate the organic nature of the perception, interpretation and classification at work in memory construction. As they write:

> Short-term memory includes forgetting as a process; it merges not with the instant but instead with the nervous, temporal, and collective rhizome. Long-term memory (family, race, society, or civilization) traces and translates, but what it translates continues to act in it, from a distance, off beat, in an 'untimely' way, not instantaneously.[17]

What this formulation also draws attention to is the fact that what is being recounted here is not a simple redrawing of the past but is, rather, an intervention into a 'now' which actively, even creatively, constitutes the past as determined by present interests. A mastery over time is asserted by the authoritarian regime which works to locate everything within recognisable and, more pertinently, retrievable systems of representations. The *struggle* over remembering or even its failure is mobilised to repress the troublesome.[18]

Therefore, what is replayed is not a metaphorical film clip or photograph retrieved from the archive of memory but a mechanism which functions, at least partly, as a re-creation. Elizabeth Loftus ruefully observes, paraphrasing the Uruguayan novelist Eduardo Galeano, that 'memory is born anew every day'.[19] We think the past from the present to construct a memory of it. For Richard Terdiman, there is a folding back on itself of the time-line between 'then' and 'now' and 'such a complication constitutes our lives and defines our experience. The complex of practices and means by which the past invests the present is memory: *memory is the present past*'.[20] There is repetition at work in memory that always involves the new and must inevitably incorporate an awareness of what is known now but was not then.

For Loftus, memory is not just determined by the parameters of time and place but is a synthesis of experiences and, centrally, becomes shaped by the social nature of communication. The first thing those involved in or witness to a traumatic event do is to begin to talk to each other, to attempt to begin to make sense of it. This does not mean that any subsequent recounting is necessarily contaminated on a scale of purity but, rather, that it is an actual part of any memory formation and is qualitatively different to the notion of a conspiracy to pervert the truth. As one of the family members recounted to Hayes and Campbell, 'people may get mixed up in relation to their memory, it's acceptable'.[21] Such an example of genuine confusion might be that of the experienced journalist David Tereshchuk, who was called as a witness to the inquiry. He recalled a very strong image from the day of a soldier who was wearing the red beret of the Parachute Regiment firing at the crowd. But evidence indicates beyond reasonable doubt that the Paras were wearing riot helmets as they engaged the crowd and not their berets. According to Loftus, whom he consulted later, he probably 'superimposed' one snapshot over another in the tumult of gunfire.[22] For Tereshchuk, this was troubling but did not alter the substantial thrust of his testimony that the shooting had been unprovoked.

But is it really useful to assert that memory and witness testimony is less about the reproduction of an original moment and more about a process of construction across time infused with lived experience? Does this introduce a kind of relativism into attempts to ascertain the truth of contested events? Can we consider memories as something fluid rather than fixed and therefore subject to change over time? What is at work, in this formulation, is a process of constant reworking rather than the notion of simply accessing a databank of fixed memories. This raises the relevance of *how* over that time memory has actually been mobilised and re-presented. Given the spectacularisation of society and the increasingly media-based imagination that informs popular and individual memory, it becomes increasingly important to consider this aspect of recall and retelling.[23] As Pierre Nora states: 'Ours is an intensely retinal and powerfully televisual memory.'[24] In this way memory itself becomes technologised and an area of contest and conflict.

Key to this process of memory across time is the role of film and television, and this is presumably why solicitors were so keen to raise the issue of the extent of witness engagement with cultural representations of the events that day. Indeed, one of the most important military witnesses, General Sir Robert Ford, asserted that any recollection he had of what he saw that day was probably actually from television and video footage he had watched over the years.

However, a formulation such as this does point to the fact that memory is unstable and always located within a conceptual framework that is inherently social. The inquiry, therefore, becomes an exercise in remembering and witnesses would need as much assistance as possible in sustaining this process. The inquiry, therefore, was not a neutral space of objective investigation but an attempt to resolve (or perhaps to re-solve) a conflict between contested identities as part of an ongoing process of reconciliation; this was, perhaps, its strength, but it was also its weakness.

The issue of identity in relation to memory and to the events of Bloody Sunday becomes important here. By any definition, what was in process at that time was a struggle over identity and the assertion of it in stark terms, whether claimed or imposed. Northern Ireland always has been a territory of competing narratives, histories and identities. The challenge to any notion of history asserted in relation to it almost immediately comes up against arguments posed in terms of memory, experience and authenticity. Mark Saville will presumably seek to present his report as a definitive account based on the vast amount of evidence presented to him, but it can never satisfy all claims to know that time by all that experienced it. But this is not to deny the possibility that a degree of certainty may be arrived at and then presented in unequivocal terms. The key question will be the extent to which the British State and its agents will be judged and held to account for its actions on the day.

As was argued in Chapter 1, one of the consequences of Bloody Sunday was the relative fixing of the conflict into more rigid, binary lines than was potentially possible. Another consequence was the subsequent high level of militarisation of the Bogside as it became a heavily policed, surveilled and hostile location for the state. For those living within it, a strong sense of place and identity would be manifestly clear. Alan Megill argues that in a context where identity is challenged memory is necessarily valorised. He writes, in response to optimistic readings of various truth commissions into state-sponsored atrocities, that

> courts and commissions seeking at the same time to discover historical truth and to reconstruct collective identity are relevant in the present context as a manifestation of the general theoretical points that I have tried to articulate. These are: (1) that the uncertainties of history, identity and memory are mutual; (2) that history and memory are sharply different, as manifested above all in the radically different histories that different people or groups 'remember'; (3) that the boundaries between history and memory nonetheless cannot be precisely established; and (4) that in the absence of a single, unquestioned authority or framework, the tension between history and memory cannot be resolved.[25]

This also draws attention to the performative nature of the inquiry, where evidence such as documented eyewitness testimony is made to speak through the subject on the stand. The notion of testimony as a performance usefully points to the ontological status of the inquiry as a live event. As Philip Auslander asserts, the essence of testimony is the performance of recollection,[26] whilst, for White, the modes of courtroom performance and acts of remembering are marked by truth effects that are powerfully affective.[27] Legal proceedings are staged as exercises in remembering and to remember ones needs others located within a coherent system of meaning and communication where to recollect is to reconstruct. It is the shift from memory as a form of knowledge to that of a form of action that opens up a space for a necessary evaluation of the notion of an *ethics* of memory. Paul Ricoeur argues:

> This is so because remembering is a way of *doing* things, not only with words, but with our minds; in remembering or recollecting we are exercising our memory, which is a kind of action. It is because memory is an exercise that we can talk of the *use* of memory, which in turn permits us to speak of the *abuses* of memory.[28]

Figure 6. The Bloody Sunday Inquiry, The Guildhall, Derry
(*Photo courtesy PA Photos*)

For Ricoeur, any potential abuse is always intrinsically linked to problems of identity and its maintenance over time. He offers two
contrasting forms of identity prefaced by Latin to distinguish them: *idem*
and *ipse*. The former is defined by enduring sameness, the latter as
strategy defined by flexibility in a changing world. Both operate in relation to the *other* as a source of threat.[29]

In the Bloody Sunday Inquiry, the large screens projecting statements
for the witnesses and the audience to view effectively dramatise the

documents for the necessary act of retelling and remembering the events they describe. The documents are made to speak through the subject on the stand to other subjects in, at the very least, an argumentative context that is directed, supposedly, towards the singular purpose of establishing the truth. The inherent tension in this process was a source of disappointment for some relatives of those killed, who felt alienated by the shift to a rather more adversarial style of questioning than they had been led to believe would be the case. For Tony Doherty, whose father was killed on Bloody Sunday, the potential for reconciliation was damaged in this process: 'the law is an imperfect vehicle for getting at the truth, particularly when dealing with national issues. It is not the best vehicle for dealing with historical injustice.'[30]

Yet Megill insists on the need for the boundary between memory and history to be sustained yet for neither to subsume the other, as truth and justice demand 'at least the ghost of History if they are to have any claim on people at all',[31] rather than just see it replaced by memory. Whatever account Saville finally comes out with will always be haunted by the memories of those who bore witness to the events that day. As Liliane Weissberg points out in this context with regard to memory:

> it is absolute, while history is relative; it claims objects, images, and space for itself, while history insists on the passing of time. As a democratic notion, it wants to belong to everyone, and negotiates between each individual and the collective.[32]

So what is the relationship between individual and collective memory? Is the former sustainable as a distinct category and, if so, under what terms? Certainly, it bears on the question of identity as something that both shapes and is shaped by collective experience and consciousness. This can be extended to memory where it functions as a process that negotiates between individual will and social context and is always directed towards a purpose.

Maurice Halbwachs' concept of collective memory, first introduced in 1925, sets out the idea that individuals always rely upon other peoples memories to confirm their own interpretations and that they persist over time. Lived experience will always be mediated through symbolic structures and social organisations, which endure as memory over time on the basis of ongoing practices of understanding, through the matrix of identity. We can see in relation to Bloody Sunday that this collective memory is cross-generational, as illustrated by the poem by Sharon Meenan and Killian Mullan, who write of 'remembering' what happened that day but conclude with the line 'And I wasn't even born'.[33] Fundamental to this concept is the originating idea of a collective consciousness, which in turn derives from the experience of the strength and will of the crowd. In Chapter 2 we discussed aspects of the formation of the crowd on Bloody Sunday and in subsequent anniversaries and commemorations, in which we emphasised the differences within it. In contrast to this, we can consider the other axis of the crowd formation and those elements of collectivity and cohesion that frame its social identity. The annual commemorations were, after the first few anniversaries, sustained by Sinn Féin up until the early 1990s, when the families began to play a more central role.[34] Graham Dawson writes of how the linking of Bloody Sunday in Derry with the longer historical struggle against British rule plays an important part in the possibility of coming to terms with such an event within a political context:

> These politicised narratives of memory offer immense psychic resources of strength, hope, and resilience to the members of the embattled communities. They provide collective, cultural means to combat the disintegration and withdrawal of the self that so often marks the presence of the traumatic.[35]

So, whilst such commemorations provide a cohesion by being read through a political register, they can then become subject to the same bitter struggles over history that marks the entire cultural geography of the region.[36]

The trauma of what happened that day was from the beginning a collective trauma. What is significant in the accounts of those who survived is the intrinsic connection between individual narratives and collective experience. The physical and inter-familial density of the area of the Bogside, Brandywell and Creggan meant that those on the march were deeply rooted in the place where the killings took place: Dawson writes of a 'traumatised community' in which thousands of people experienced a similar traumatic experience which affected them, and to which they responded, in a shared collective way.[37] Every year since Bloody Sunday there has been a restaging of the march and, over time, the establishment of events and public fora that have opened up the focus of the demonstration to one that raises questions about human rights and the future of the region rather than simply functioning as a memorial to an injustice. In between times what sustains the continuing sense of collective identity has been a topography of sanctified places that, as Halbwachs states, 'binds our most intimate remembrances to each other'.[38] This inter-relationship between place, subject and memory can clearly be seen in the Bogside, with its large gable-end murals, monuments (*lieux de mémoire*, to use Pierre Nora's phrase) and demarcated boundaries of overbearing city walls. This 'cultural landscape', as Dawson calls it, run through with stories and practices of remembrance, enables a community and the individuals within it to orient themselves socially and psychically: 'The concept of imaginative geography points to the interconnections between these cultural and political processes and the psychic and emotional dimensions of attachment and identification.'[39] Collective memory, therefore, is a multimedia collage and the technology of the Saville inquiry was, in part at least, an attempt to dismantle it.

We can also place the Saville inquiry in relation to the temporal registers of experience, memory and futures. The inquiry was an exercise in retrieving the past, to satisfy the demand for justice now, and in making possible a different future, defined as not the repetition of the past. As Rafel Narvaez observes: 'Collective memory is not only about remembering (the past) or about social order and action (the present), but, critically, it is about how social groups project themselves towards the future.'[40] Whether the final outcome of the Saville Inquiry creates favourable conditions for the looking-forward to shared and inherited futures is still, at this point, uncertain.

Virtual reality

> . . . some of the people who have come forward to the inquiry have been emotionally affected by the software. In many respects it has brought back the ghosts of what happened.[41]

One of the most striking features of the Saville inquiry has been its extensive use of information technology. All evidence submitted to the inquiry (whether written, photographic, audio or physical) was digitised, to enable convenient access to it in the day-to-day hearings. As witnesses gave their testimony, their original statements to the inquiry team were displayed on large screens with their relevant passages highlighted, acting as both an *aide-mémoire* and as a tool of cross-examination. Not only did the use of TrialPro Evidence Display System enable all participants in the inquiry to see the identical information at the same time, it also fed information to audiences viewing the proceedings in 'satellite' locations across the city of Derry: the Rialto Cinema and the offices of the Bloody Sunday Trust, for example. Similarly, all the proceedings were recorded using LiveNote Real-Time Transcription, so that statements and misunderstanding could be clarified within seconds. This technology also allowed the Bloody Sunday inquiry website to carry verbatim transcripts of every moment of the proceedings. While the inquiry's website did not, as originally intended, display each item of evidence, every submission was available for viewing to all participants via their computer terminals. This publication and broadcasting of evidence was in marked contrast to the 1972 investigation, when the proceedings and evidence became available only after the tribunal had ended (and at a price of £150).

At the heart of the inquiry was the virtual reality (VR) imaging system, which enabled eyewitnesses to recall their memories of the event by leading them through a re-creation of the Bogside as it looked in 1972. This 'virtual' Bogside, developed by Malachy McDaid of the

Northern Ireland Council for Curriculum, Examinations and Assessment (CCEA) using Apple QuickTime, is Saville's version of the cardboard model deployed in the Widgery tribunal. Counsel for Saville, Christopher Clarke, QC, made reference to these models:

> Lord Widgery's Inquiry made use of a very large model of the relevant area. We have tried to see whether that model, of which we only possess photographs, still exists and, if so, to find it. Our present understanding is that the model may have been manufactured by the RAF's Modelling Department, but that it probably no longer exists. If anybody has any contrary information, the Tribunal would like to hear of it. We have been, accordingly, considering whether, for the purposes of the full hearing, we should commission another model. With the aid of modern technology, it is now possible to create on a computer what is, in effect, a three-dimensional model of any given location at any given time, provided that sufficient data from photographs, plans and the like are available for that purpose.[42]

The reason why a model of some sort was necessary was that the physical environment of the Bogside has, over the past thirty years, changed quite substantially. The Rossville Flats have been demolished; William Street, once filled with factories (such as Richardson's shirt factory, Stevenson's Bakery) and other light industry, is now largely a residential

Figure 7. Virtual Reality, The Bloody Sunday Inquiry, Rossville street
(*Photo courtesy Malachy McDaid*)

area; and the terraces of tiny houses around Free Derry Wall have disappeared. Lord Saville and the developers of this virtual Derry insist
that its function is to assist in memory recall, to orient eyewitnesses and
participants in a time and a place some three decades distant. The
designer of the system insists, too, on the memory-jogging function of
this piece of technology.

These views of the virtual software as a passive *aide-mémoire* accord
with the 'traditional' role of technology in court or tribunal proceedings,
the aim of which is to aid the smooth running of the judicial or investigative process. In the UK and Ireland we are unused to seeing televised
recordings or live transmissions of court proceedings, unless, of course,
they are being televised from a celebrity trial in the United States. It
would be fair, therefore, to describe the lengths to which Saville has
gone to make *visible* the investigative and the inquisitorial processes of
the inquiry as a highly significant intervention, not just in terms of dis-
covering the truth about Bloody Sunday itself, but also in the wider
context of the legitimacy of civil law in post-ceasefire Northern Ireland.
Lord Widgery's report was an instance where the discursive violence of
the British state was seen by many as almost more painful than the
actual violence of the bullets fired on that day; Edward Daly's memorable comment about Widgery as the second atrocity, in which 'the
innocent were found to be guilty – the guilty found to be innocent',
neatly articulates the views of many Derry nationalists/Catholics.
Saville, therefore, needed to be seen to respond fulsomely and actively to
the demands of the families' campaign for an inquiry that was open,
wide-ranging and independent. Judging by many of the comments of the
Bloody Sunday families, these demands and expectations seem, to
varying degrees, to have been met.

Given the length of time since the events of Bloody Sunday, the
primary motivation for the virtual reality environment was the need to
allow witnesses to locate themselves in the original spaces of the Bogside
and to confirm their testimony of what they remembered seeing and
hearing on that day. In an interview with the author, Malachy McDaid
described the lengths to which the design team went to accurately render
the contemporary landscape and built environment of the Bogside. The
verisimilitude of the imaging was achieved by cross-referencing against a
series of photographs – some held by Derry City Council archives and
others submitted to the inquiry by news organisations, freelance photographers and members of the public. Very few architectural plans were
available for the area, and, ironically perhaps, there was no recent map
of the Bogside; the most up-to-date was based on the Northern Ireland
Ordnance Survey of 1948. As a Bogsider himself, McDaid relied on personal and family memories to enhance certain features of the VR:
pebble-dashing on the front of maisonettes; a patch of garden by the
entrance to a flat in Glenfada Park.

Figure 8. Virtual Reality, The Bloody Sunday Inquiry, the Rubble Barricade, Rossville Street (*Photo courtesy Malachy McDaid*)

The difference between this virtual reality assistant and the cardboard model used in the Widgery tribunal is the *immersive* nature of the VR model. Witnesses could indicate via a touchscreen where they were standing as the shooting started; in what direction they moved thereafter; what they could see and hear from their hiding places. True VR environments are, of course, experienced through a headset and movement simulated with sensors on hands and legs. However, the VR environment at the Saville inquiry was limited by the practicalities of viewing a computer screen while at the same time being able to give testimony or withstand cross-examination. Ease of use was facilitated by a screen rather than mouse or trackpad: the designers of the system were aware that many people appearing at the inquiry would have little or no experience of using computers. Witnesses could position themselves by use of the initial map screen, then be able to turn 360 degrees on one of the 84 'hotspots' to visually experience the 3D environment and indicate what they had seen and heard. The true-to-scale nature of the 3D landscape meant that if someone had testified, for instance, that they were standing in one spot and saw a gunman on the roof of a building, this could be tested by looking at that building to see if it was in fact possible to see such a detail. The 3D landscape was overlaid with contemporary photographs mapped onto modelling software, and at times an artist's impression was deployed to fill in any gaps, with an inevitable element of artistic licence at work. There is no doubt that this ambitious system provided a powerful 'prompt' to the memory of any individual witness. As a neutral environment (it was devoid of people) and subject to the prior approval of all parties to the inquiry, the landscape produced in this virtual environment was agreed by those parties to be a faithful rendering of the Bogside as it existed in January 1972. In other words, this landscape was closely aligned to the 'real', to what (people felt or remembered) had once been real. Almost every witness at the inquiry made use of the software; in short, it became a central component of the Bloody Sunday inquiry.

Beyond the inquiry the VR system was highly praised; indeed, it won the 2001 Europrix prize for 'Empowering Citizens and Improving Democracy with Multimedia'. For some commentators it was indicative of the way in which technology in a legal setting could be employed to provide clarity for every possible kind of dispute.[43] Such faith seems slightly ill-conceived, more indicative of a utopian imaginary akin to a Star Trek 'holodeck', with its possibility of complete re-creation of any given environment from the past by an omniscient computer. What seems to be forgotten is that, as Sean Doran observes, the general layout of the Bogside is not really in dispute – it's what happened there that is contested. He observes, 'there is surely some irony in the employment of this technique in the present context: a case of the camera lying in order to get at the truth'.[44] Naive belief in the impartiality of technology should be rejected in favour of a rather more rigorous awareness of the long history of miscarriages of justice founded upon the so-called application of science enacted by individual agents grounded in a legal discourse.

A virtual reality is not a re-creation but a construction and therefore subject to the potential biases of any such socially based interpretation. One of the first applications of such VR technology since the Saville inquiry was an attempt by the Metropolitan Police to solve the murder of PC Keith Blakelock during the Tottenham riots in 1985. According to a BBC online-news report: 'The virtual reality reconstruction of the murder scene will allow detectives to picture the Broadwater Farm estate as it was in 1985.'[45] Given the re-opening of the case due to the successful appeals of those originally convicted for this crime because of the suspicion that evidence had been fabricated, care should be taken when championing any kind of technology as providing some kind of angelic re-creation.

Justice

In the epigraph that opened this chapter Lyotard makes reference to the 'perfect crime' as one that obtains the silence of the victims, the deafness of the judges and the exposure laid before him of the inconsistency of testimony of the witnesses. Lord Widgery was indeed deaf to much of the evidence and efforts were certainly made to present the witnesses' testimony as inconsistent and flawed. However, the silence of the victims and those around them was not so easily obtained. The longstanding call for justice was a defence of the dead; a remembering that was defined by an ethic of responsibility. The lie propounded about the victims that day was a form of appropriation of the dead for political ends by the forces of the state. Justice for them has been, at least partly, a reclaiming by those in whose name they had acted. Derrida writes of this process:

> If I am getting ready to speak at length about ghosts, inheritance, and generations, generations of ghosts, which is to say about certain *others* who are not present, nor presently living, either to us, in us, or outside us, it is in the name of *justice* . . . No justice . . . seems possible or thinkable without the principle of some *responsibility*, beyond all living present, within that which disjoins the living present, before the ghosts of those who are not yet born or who are already dead, be they victims of wars, political or other kinds of violence, nationalist, racist, colonialist, sexist, or other kinds of exterminations, victims of the oppressions of capitalist imperialism or any of the forms of totalitarianism.[46]

The memory work that sustains the demand is one that is never complete and justice can never be ultimately achieved. But this is not to deny the possibility of *just acts*. As Ricoeur observes, amnesty cannot be based on amnesia, and we are only at the beginning of implementing a culture of *just memory*.[47] In the case of the Saville inquiry into Bloody Sunday, the specificities of any such outcome are yet to be seen but it is perhaps doubtful that the ghosts will be resolutely and completely laid to rest.

4

Repetition and Restaging
Bloody Sunday as
Drama-Documentary

In every respect, repetition is a transgression. It puts law into question, it denounces its nominal or general character in favour of a more profound and more artistic reality.[1]

Introduction

The transmission on British television of two drama-documentaries, *Bloody Sunday* and *Sunday*, to coincide with the thirtieth anniversary of Bloody Sunday was of enormous importance in raising awareness of the event outside of Derry and, in a different way, offered the families and community some kind of validation for their long and largely lonely insistence on a counter-history to that of the Widgery Report. If the Saville inquiry could be characterised as a 'document-drama', 'drama-documentary' worked on a quite different register.

In the previous ten years there had been a number of films made from a documentary perspective, such as the Derry filmmaker Margo Harkin's *The Bloody Sunday Murders*, the award-winning journalist Peter Taylor's investigation, *Remember Bloody Sunday*, which was notable for the confessional nature of some of the testimony by military personnel, and British television Channel 4's news inserts based upon Don Mullan's work on how some of the victims could have been shot by snipers positioned on the City Walls overlooking the Bogside, which qualified as 'new evidence' on the day. All of these documentary-style investigations played a part in making visible the campaign for a new legitimate inquiry into the events of Bloody Sunday. The two drama-based films, therefore, sought to work on a level of human interest and freely defined characterisation. Between them, however, there was a stark contrast in the method of production that raises important questions.

Jimmy McGovern's production *Sunday* went to great lengths to involve many people from the area, both as background, through extensive interviews and consultation, and as foreground, by casting a number of young relatives of the victims as the individuals on screen. This can be seen as part of an established strategy developed by McGovern going back to *Hillsborough*, with its similar concerns to give voice to the experiences of grieving families ill-served by official discourse. Paul Greengrass adopted a quite different approach to the subject, mobilising a different range of documentary effects. A consideration of these differences highlights a number of important conceptual issues about restaging an event such as Bloody Sunday and the consequent negotiation of trauma, memory and history. By grounding the narratives in the evidential status of the documentary but at the same time mobilising the creative aspects of dramatisation, such a production opens up a potentially critical space for the articulation of different histories and, to varying degrees, reflects upon the difficulties of any such strategy.

McGovern's extensive engagement with the families and community of Derry gave visibility to a range of experiences of Bloody Sunday long ignored by official history. In this sense the process by which the final televisual film (directed by Charles McDougall and produced by Gub Neal) was arrived at seemed, at times, almost as important as what appeared on screen. Indeed, McGovern has written of this in a discussion of the approach he took to the film: 'Another rule I stick to: the process of writing a drama-doc is as important as the drama-doc itself. It must empower the powerless.'[2] Such a strategy should not be underestimated, providing, as it does, an affirmative and cathartic experience for the community or individuals involved. It also provides a huge amount of potentially dramatic material from which to identify the eventual storyline. The film's website sets out in detail the lengths the production team went to to establish an accurate and engaged drama:

> The programme, made with the full consultation and co-operation of the families affected by the tragedy, has been carefully researched over several years by an experienced factual production team. More than a hundred first-hand interviews have been conducted with British soldiers and officers, priests, politicians, medical experts and eyewitnesses as well as relatives.
> . . . Gaslight Productions was formed to research and develop the story. McGovern wrote the script based on interviews with the bereaved and wounded, and soldiers, as well as a wide cross-section of people involved on the day.
> A team of investigative journalists, led by Factual Producer Katy Jones, also conducted painstaking background research for the programme, and corroborated the factual basis of the drama-documentary independently. Key scenes are based on evidence presented to the Widgery and Saville inquiries.[3]

Jimmy McGovern's film tells the story from the perspective of the families and for this reason alone was warmly welcomed by the people of the Bogside and Creggan. McGovern uses his signature style and approach to construct a story defined by the codes of television drama and the intimacies of scale deriving from domestic narratives. It is worth considering in detail some of the strategies he employs to construct his account of the event.

At the very beginning, in the opening credits, he assures the viewer of the veracity and documentary truth of the film:

> This film is a dramatised reconstruction
> of events between 1968 and 1973.
> Although there have been minor changes to
> chronology and certain events have been
> dramatised to aid clarity, this drama is based
> entirely on fact using British Government
> documents, interviews, eyewitness reports
> and court transcripts.[4]

This fades into the opening scenes of the film, drawn from archive footage of the civil rights movement, before starting the film proper as it reveals the face of Leo Young, whose emotional journey we then follow through the course of the film. As we follow him on his rounds as a coal-delivery man, he provides the voice-over:

> The coal man gave me the job. I was grateful for it. 'Cos this was Derry in '68. Britain was booming, Europe was booming but Derry was on the dole. I was lucky I was working.
>
> That's a businessman, a Protestant. In '68 he owned a company so he got 6 votes. But this was the Duddy family. The family only had one property so they only got 1 vote between them all. So in 1968 we marched for jobs, houses and the right to vote. And this is what the world saw on its TV screens.
>
> The RUC attacked Sammy Deveney. Sammy died. The Bogside erupted. Free Derry was born. The British Army came in and the IRA campaign began. Just as a girl from Derry was winning the Eurovision song contest.
>
> In 1971 the army killed two local people, Seamus Cussack and Dessie Beattie, strengthening support for the IRA. So the Government introduced Internment, imprisonment without trial. There were wee riots every day.

Through this voice-over and the dialogue of the characters on screen in this initial section, clearly the intention is to present, however briefly, a historical context for what is about to happen on the march proper. Again, for many this attempt to contextualise and identify the political and military pressures that are seen is key to being able to explain what happened on Bloody Sunday and why. Presumably the impetus for this is to provide an explanation for viewers outside of Derry and the North of Ireland who might be unfamiliar with the history of the period leading up to Bloody Sunday itself. Paradoxically, for some it was rather better received in Derry than elsewhere, expressing, as it does, a precious counter-history to official accounts of the time and decades of simplistic media analysis. The perceived strength of the narrative, stretching over a five-year period, is to explain Bloody Sunday as one event amongst others, and therefore understandable in relation to them. We will return to this aspect of the films later on in the chapter.

Paul Greengrass approached the subject differently, framing his account within a classical 24-hour period. His filmic technique adopts the free-flowing aesthetic of hand-held cameras and strong ambient sound that produces a powerful documentary effect. He takes as his central character the civil rights leader Ivan Cooper, played by the well-known actor James Nesbitt. This is not an insignificant detail, as it provides, firstly, a platform for a wider audience attracted and engaged by the capable performance of the popular actor, and, secondly, it provides a connection with the location of Derry, as Nesbitt himself was born and brought up in a Protestant family in nearby Coleraine. Basing the story on a Protestant civil rights leader gave useful insights into the period but simultaneously raised other concerns. As Eamonn McCann commented:

> It is right that Cooper should be given back a prominent place in the events of the day and the period surrounding it. He has been rather written out of the history, mostly because he left front-line politics a few years later. However, one problem with telling the story through his eyes is that it requires him to be placed at the heart of events throughout. Bending the stick back in order to straighten it, writer-director Paul Greengrass has come close to breaking it.[5]

Greengrass characterises his film as a 'drama based on documentary evidence', as opposed to a straight drama-doc. Rather than prefacing the film, as McGovern does, with a statement of truth, he closes with the statement that:

> This film is based on true events.
> However, certain details, dialogue, scenes and characters
> have been invented or adapted
> in the process of dramatising the film.[6]

This reflects a contrasting tone to that of the McGovern film. By the way in which its filmic codes are organised *Bloody Sunday* presents a much more fractured filmic experience than that of McGovern's *Sunday*, who is concerned to *explain* more than just *show*. A criticism levelled at the Greengrass film is its failure to visibly identify the political manoeuvring that led up to the atrocity, characterised by one critic as adopting the 'cock-up theory' as opposed to the 'conspiracy theory' of the day. Indeed, when Greengrass uses many of the same strategies in his film *United 93* and its almost real-time portrayal of the hijacking and crashing of the fourth plane on 11 September 2001, the cultural theorist Slavoj Žižek criticises his approach for its failure to provide 'cognitive mapping' for the actions of those involved, and therefore failing to take a necessary political stance.[7] However, this draws attention to an important concern for such a cultural intervention: the role of the viewer in his or her own negotiation of the text. An appropriate phrase to describe this might be Paul De Man's notion of blindness and insight, where one mode of reading, whilst providing illumination in one way, cannot but work to exclude as an originating locus, in another.[8] Martin McLoone writing in the journal *Cineaste* points to this when he observes of *Bloody Sunday*: 'The irony is that, in its pursuit of documentary realism and immediacy, in its wonderfully evocative re-creation of live history, it perhaps disguises the truth as much as it reveals reality.'[9] Any revelation one way will always in another way disguise and so be open to criticism in those excluded terms. John Hill in his book on cinema in Northern Ireland has written of how the strategy of mapping political tensions onto family dilemmas in films such as *In the Name of the Father* (1993) subordinates the complexities of the politics at work to the modes of melodrama figured around the family.[10] Indeed, Hill also suggests that by focusing on individuals and the drama within the family relationships there is a tendency, evident in films such as *Hidden Agenda* (1990), for instance, towards conspiracy theories concerning the role of the British state.[11]

It can be argued that *Sunday* constructs a very narrow space for the viewer, filling in all the gaps and pulling the viewer along a tightly defined path towards a moment of closure. By contrast, in *Bloody Sunday* the viewers are not offered such a secure sense of their own location. As the film opens, the camera follows Cooper into a press conference, where he outlines the historical basis for the march itself, rooted in Britain's colonial involvement and the statelet's structures of discrimination. This points to a key issue when constructing the film narrative: where to begin? Greengrass writes in the 'Forward' to Don Mullan's republished *Eyewitness Bloody Sunday* about the problem of finding such a starting-point for the film:

> But how to tell it – where should we begin? Early January 1972 when the march was conceived? With the introduction of Internment in the summer of 1971? The start of the Civil Rights Movement in 1968? Partition in 1921? The Siege of Derry? Tracing the roots of Bloody Sunday was an endless journey into the mists of history.[12]

So any strategy of recounting the historical event must immediately seek to draw lines between what is relevant and what is, arguably, less relevant. Within the context of the history of Ireland, and specifically the north, such decisions are used to fix the interpretation in an already established political framework. But the demand is for a representation of the event. Hayden White points to the difficulties inherent in this:

> . . . any attempt to provide an objective account of the event, either by breaking it up into a mass of its details or by setting it within its context, must conjure with two circumstances: one is that the number of details identifiable in any singular event is potentially infinite; and the other is that the 'context' of any singular event is infinitely extensive or at least is not objectively determinable.[13]

Perhaps a useful distinction would be that between a notion of origin and of a beginning. With *Sunday* we are offered a way into the drama by something closer to the mythical idea of origin, whereas in *Bloody Sunday* what is presented is less an origin and more a sense of a necessary beginning, a distinction critically evaluated by Edward Said: 'A beginning gives us the chance to do work that compensates us for the tumbling disorder of brute reality that will not settle down.'[14]

Paul Greengrass takes a different tack to Jimmy McGovern and establishes a dynamic to the narrative structure by framing the event with the contested assertions of moral grounding for the actions about to take place. There is a rhythm to *Bloody Sunday* that is established in the opening frames as we switch between the two counterposed political/ institutional zones of, firstly, the civil rights leader Ivan Cooper, played by James Nesbitt, and secondly, General Ford, played by Tim Pigott-Smith. The hand-held camera echoes the walking rhythm of the character it follows into the meeting where the press conference is to be held. The voice of Cooper is audible as we follow him through the crowd. So a documentary style is mobilised to create a sense of actuality. The screen fades to black and then opens on the row of army officers gathered around Ford as he is announced. By fading the screen to black Greengrass gives a powerful sense of the incompatibility of the different positions of the spokesmen of two organisations in conflict, as the blackness conveys a sense of chasmic distance between them.

Through the contrasting assertions of the characters the primary conflict is revealed. On the one hand there is the historically rooted demand for civil rights (voiced by Cooper), starkly and effectively posed against an insistence on the absolute authority of the rule of law: 'the law is the law and *must* be respected' (Ford). The rhythm is audibly produced by a contrasting drumbeat: firstly of the civil rights campaign, with a *bodhrán* and its free-flowing form, and secondly of the military drumroll, with its order and regimented timing, a cinematic-audio signifier well established in films on the conflict in Ireland. On the wall behind Cooper, McCann and Devlin is the civil rights banner; behind Ford and his staff is a large-scale map gridded and coded for military surveillance. Greengrass makes use of ambient sound throughout his film to strip back the finished style of conventional drama and produce an effect of everyday-like babble and messy interruptions. From this point on what is apparent is the ongoing fracturing, or splintering as one commentator puts it,[15] of the characters and viewpoints.

This opening is in contrast to McGovern's voice-over, which comes from off-screen and provides a historical context but also presumes a particular model of the viewer. Mary Ann Doane writes of this process:

> The means by which sound is deployed in the cinema inplicate [*sic*] the spectator in a particular textual problematic – they establish certain conditions for understanding which obtain in the 'intersubjective relation' between film and spectator. The voiceover commentary and, differently, the interior monologue and voiceover flashback speak more or less *directly* to the spectator, constituting him/her as an empty space to be 'filled' with knowledge about events, character psychology, etc.[16]

The voice is anchored in the body of Leo Young as he goes about his labours and the film roots itself in his emotional landscape and his journey through the experience of the day and its aftermath.

Event

There is no doubt that in different ways both films powerfully express the appalling trauma of the events of that day, from the shootings to the scenes in the hospital morgue, what McCann refers to as 'the moral truth of the Derry Massacre'.[17] But how far do the films move towards or away from Bloody Sunday as an event? We want to consider this aspect of both films to tentatively think about what happened and how it is reactivated within a cinematic framework. It is often asserted that the establishment of a final and singular truth of what happened on that day will allow for a process of closure and resolution, and perhaps for those involved such an aspiration is understandable. But there is a danger that what is being pursued is something which will ultimately smooth over the actual and very real inconsistencies, partialities and blank spots of an event such as this. This is not to deny, as has been said, the moral truth of what happened that day and the innocence of those killed. Rather, in different ways, the two films produce differing perspectives on the process of interpretation and sense-making that must take place *after* the event.

Over the last decades there has been much consideration and theorisation of narrative as literary device and its hegemonic function. Essential, then, is a reflection upon the tension between an understanding of the event as something fundamentally irruptive and narrative as a historicist device. Firstly, let us consider the question of temporality in relation to this and the chronology of the narrative structure. Joanne O'Brien refers to the event in this way when she titles her book *A Matter of Minutes*. We are used to living with an understanding of time as a sequence of discrete and uniform moments that lead in one direction. What the event points to is a moment when such familiarities are brutally shaken and perception, understanding and experience cannot be accommodated within this context. Everyone who speaks of that day from the marchers' perspective makes reference to the initial confusion, based on utter disbelief at the reality of the Paratroopers firing round after round of live ammunition into the bodies of fleeing panic-stricken civilians, and this is a quality both films communicate well.

What can be seen to operate, therefore, is the inherent tension of articulating in a historical form an event that is in this sense, by definition, outside history, outside of narrativisation. Indeed, for the French philosopher Jean-François Lyotard there is a violence done to the very nature of the event when it becomes located within the closed structure of narrative; as he puts it, 'Narratives drive the event back to the border.'[18] For him the achronological effect of the event is precisely a consequence of the shock of the unassimilatable trauma.[19]

The understanding of the event as a bifurcation, as discussed in Chapter 1, points to the ongoing tension within it, between the polarities of open/closed. Arguably, *Bloody Sunday* tends far more to articulating the open nature of the event than McGovern's rather more closed narrative structure. As Derrida argues, the basis on which we act to recognise an event as *event* is that it will always endure beyond attempts to cogently narrativise it.[20] The trauma of the event is driven by its irruptive nature, which, whilst needing to be inserted into any number of narratives, such as personal, historical or political, ultimately resists any final closure. As the event manifests itself through the range of discursive and dramatic repetitions, it still oscillates between the illegibility of the trauma of the real and an increasing level of narrativisation. The spectrality of the event is the return of that which was not able to be said. Yet the inscription is what allows for any sense of the event occurring at all, as Laura Marks writes of intercultural cinema: 'A film can recreate, not the true historical event, but at least another version of it, by searching into the discursive layers in which it was found.'[21] Marks defines this by turning to Deleuze, who writes in *Cinema 2*:

> History is inseparable from the earth [*terre*], struggle is underground [*sous terre*], and, if we want to grasp an event we must not show it, we must not pass along the event, but plunge into it, go through all the geological layers that are its internal history (and not simply a more or less distant past).[22]

There will always, in this way, be an excess, which is why trauma is understood as a wound inflicted upon the mind and not just the body. Cathy Caruth refers to the struggle within survivors to accommodate both the reality of violence of the event and the violence not yet fully known. She argues that trauma is not locatable in the simple violent or original event in an individual's past, but rather in the way that its very unassimilated nature – the way it was precisely *not known* in the first instance – returns to haunt the survivor later on.[23]

This particular sense of the experience of an event points to a number of issues that bear upon any strategy of a presentation of it. The first is that the event as such is never over and can never be complete. It is not a matter of the level of material gathered in relation to it or accuracy of testimony or witness of it. Rather, it is that it lies elsewhere than in the material support which can claim to have produced it. All the elements gathered together, however comprehensively, do not add up to the shattering singularity of the event. This can be seen within the two films in the struggle to identify the correct parameters of the event: one day, five years, fifty years and so on. As was discussed earlier, the period was one dense with possibilities and outcomes not realised, so that what can be seen is less a singular teleology than a dynamic zone of potentialities, one attractor of which was armed violence. *Sunday* tends to present the day as one of a series of days, from before, through and after, ultimately returning back to the point of origin and neatly closing the circle. *Bloody Sunday*, on the other hand, provides, we would argue, a far more effective sense of the always-in-process nature of the event. This is most effectively communicated in the ways in which the Cooper character is played through the course of the film, beginning with a clearly defined purpose and ontological grounding to his actions in organising the march, through the confusion and trauma of the shootings and the experience of attending the morgue, until ultimately he comes to a point close to muteness. There are no words that can articulate that which is beyond the realm of comprehension. As Lecercle notes, the actors in the midst of the event do not experience it as the event, as a single identity, even though the event is inherent in all of their actions.[24] The event is always in excess of the scene of the event, which goes beyond the predicted situation, what Badiou calls 'a supplement'.[25] The event, in this sense, happens because of history, yet goes beyond history, as Deleuze and Guattari write:

> What History grasps of the event is its effectuation in states of affairs or in lived experience, but the event in its becoming, in its specific consistency, in its self-positing as concept, escapes History.[26]

This aspect of the voice within the trauma raises important issues about the legibility of the event through narrative and the unassimilatable aspect generated by the inexplicable nature of the void it opens up. The attempt to ground oneself in this void is almost impossible and becomes visible in the very struggle even to describe what happened. From any judicial point of view it also becomes the basis on which to discredit the witnesses, as blanks, inconsistencies and errors are ruthlessly paraded by counsel for the military (authoritarian) regime. In this there can be no recognition of the gap between remembering and forgetting, of a temporal *lapse*, for that is potentially destabilising of the representational economy itself.

Whereas in *Sunday* the point of return is to some kind of normality, as Leo Young goes back to work (although, of course, profoundly changed), in *Bloody Sunday* Ivan Cooper is led away reduced and broken, unable to communicate the traumatic nature of what has happened. Perhaps, in itself, this is not necessarily that surprising, but what Greengrass does so well is to give a powerful sense of the need to try to do so. Once again Devlin, Cooper and McCann sit for a press conference and attempt to convey to the audience of press and journalists the enormity of what has happened in terms of the loss of individual lives but also the loss of the unique strategy for social change represented not simply by the civil rights movement but the kind of dialogue it encapsulated. This silencing, the inability to be able to express the sense of injury and injustice, is, of course, more fundamentally effected by the Widgery Report. Again, in *Sunday* this is shown but in *Bloody Sunday* it is merely referenced in the closing credits. The triumvirate is complete as political, military and finally judicial establishments shut down this troublesome enclave of dissent. But it is what *Bloody Sunday* doesn't show or narrate that has a potential beyond that of *Sunday*, as Lance Pettitt observes: 'The action of the film takes place over one day, but lots is left out, and the end of the film is inconclusive, open-ended, *un*resolved.'[27] Of course, for many this might indeed be understood as a weakness, but it is precisely this quality of stammering, of speaking with involuntary pauses or repetitions, that marks the point of suffering, of an injustice that can barely be spoken even as it demands to be. Lyotard describes this in relation to his concept the *différend* or, in other words,

> the unstable state and instant of language wherein something which must be able to be put into phrases cannot yet be. This state includes silence, which is a negative phrase, but it also calls upon phrases which are in principle possible. This state is signalled by what one ordinarily calls a feeling: 'One cannot find the words.'[28]

The press conference serves to exemplify the struggle to articulate the tension between understanding and experience as it shows the first stammering attempts to locate the events of the day through the different strata of violence at work. In contrast, the smooth and seemingly effortless presentation by the British officer installs the official account to the public domain whilst the people of the Bogside and Creggan are left, at that point, almost speechless with grief and incomprehension. Cooper introduces this first attempt at description by immediately locating what has happened in relation to other massacres: Amritsar and Sharpeville in particular. This functions to locate what has just happened as the *same* but *different* and exemplifies the aporetic struggle over meaning, shifting the strategy from one of representation to that of repetition through a staging of the interruption to intelligibility, before this gap is necessarily filled by other speakers. Amongst other things it points to differing relations to temporality, where the tragedy of Bloody Sunday is the forcible reinsertion of the struggle in Northern Ireland back into the narrative of the dominant and the loss of faith in the potential future, a future different from that which has existed. Greengrass's film manifests the experience of the return of that moment of the sense of loss, not just of life, but of the ability to convince others of the potential for a new social configuration beyond the confinements of state binary thinking. As has been argued by Luke Gibbons, the unfinished nature of political events in Ireland presents a difficulty for achieving narrative closure.[29]

Repetition

A useful comparison of the processes involved in the different restagings and filmings of Bloody Sunday can be made with the work by Jeremy Deller and his 2001 *The Battle of Orgreave* project. This was a partial re-enactment of a confrontation between British police and picketing miners that was seen as referencing one of the most important events of the 1980s during the conflict between the Conservative government, under the leadership of Margaret Thatcher, and the trades unions. Deller's project had many useful aspects, but a number of key points in the process of engaging, staging and re-enacting the event point to similar points of reference in the Bloody Sunday films. Firstly, there is a continuity of experience as many of those present on the day of the event are involved again in the restaging. Bringing together people who had been on the march and ex-British soldiers produces a palpable sense of tension, not just in the final version of the film but also, as Don Mullan describes in the commentary on the UK DVD, amongst the actors on set. Simon Mann as Colonel Wilford, the para commander, provides a convincingly authentic portrayal of the roles expected for the troops on the day. Those fragments of the actual become mobilised, to varying degrees of success between the two films, as traces of the traumatic illegibility of the event. Katie Kitamura, in an article analysing the processes at work within Deller's piece, articulates the dynamic relationship between the event and the structuring mechanism of the non-event:

> What finally characterises an event is not simply its original unforeseen and irruptive quality, but precisely this enduring tension between opening and closure, between the continued evocation of the 'real' event and the more rigid declaration of the 'non-event'. The historical event endures through that very tension, through the

paradoxical combination of continued viability and growing historical legibility.[30]

This formulation highlights the ongoing struggle over the event as it is
compelled to be located within a narrative yet is still resistant to those
very processes. The shock of the event lies precisely in its unfolding
nature beyond the immediate comprehension of those caught up in it:
utter disbelief that this could be happening amidst the confusion generated by the unimaginable becoming manifest. As an event it is the
uncertain point at which everything changes and perhaps, in this sense,
Bloody Sunday is even an anti-event, a point of halting a process of
potential change and a hardening in the sense of fixing a conflict around
narrow and antagonistic positions. Both films, therefore, sustain their
truth through a rigorous fidelity to the cataclysmic nature of what happened through the active involvement of those who bore witness to it.

A connection can be forged between Deller's work and Northern
Ireland through the work of the artist Willie Doherty. Doherty was
born in Derry and the city's landscapes have been a recurrent theme in
his work. As one who was a child in the Bogside during Bloody Sunday,
his subsequent concern to negotiate the complex relationships between
places, events, images, memory and mediatisation of the province is
central to his art practice. Carolyn Christov-Bakargiev sees both Deller
and Doherty as exploring the relationship between personal experience
and social reality.[31] Precisely what is foregrounded in Doherty's work is
the gap, elided within mass media, between experience and representation, reality and the limitations of language and image, something he
himself locates in his own sense of the unreliability of how Bloody
Sunday was represented in the media. As has been argued throughout
this chapter, the emphasis on indeterminacy and *ongoing* struggle over
meaning rather than the reassuring comforts of closure is not the same
thing as a denial of meaning or a disabling relativism. By opening up a
critical space on these processes Doherty creates an invaluable opportunity for reflection on the intransigence of media representations of
the conflict and its reductive binaries through, what Andrew Quick
refers to as the dynamics of fracture and dislocation in Doherty's
photographic work.[32]

In 1993 Doherty produced an installation entitled *30th January
1972*. It consisted of one side of a projected black-and-white 35mm slide
of gathered demonstrators taken from the television news coverage of
the day and an extract of a sound recording made during the period of
shooting. Juxtaposed with this is a colour slide from 1993 of one of the
places where people had been shot dead in 1972. Edited recordings of
interviews accompanied this with people asked questions about their
experiences of the day, if they were there, or to recall any photographic
or media images, if they were not. The contamination of memory by
images and recollections from multiple sources is, for Doherty,

something to be considered openly rather than to be used to challenge the fallibility of individual testimony. In this work and others, such as *How it Was* from 2001, there is a concern with issues of staging and restaging that attempts an interrogation of the active nature of witness testimony, memory and trauma and the incompleteness of this entire process. Christov-Bakargiev claims thus:

> His photographs and his audio/video work are partial, incomplete: they are disrupted, opaque visions, suggesting a 'disabled' gaze, eco-logically (and ethically) frozen or interrupted at the borders of privacy. Doherty thus posits a form of 'weak subjectivity': his gaze does not penetrate, nor does it go beyond a surface.[33]

Central to the assertion of identity within Northern Ireland is a certain kind of repetition: the repetition of a mythical moment that grounds the symbolic struggle for the present. As was discussed in Chapter 2, loyalist marches and parades certainly function to assert a contemporary identity through the mimicry of a military re-enactment across a set route. Northern Catholics, on the other hand, have tradi-tionally been unified around a shared sense of victimhood and a 'culture of grievance', as Marianne Elliott describes it.[34] Arguably, therefore, what distinguishes the repetition of the loyalist tradition from the repe-tition of Bloody Sunday is the former as a repetition of the same but the latter a repetition of that which cannot be represented but only repeated: a repetition of the singular. Ricoeur observes of the mobilisation of one as opposed to the other: 'Here we may say that the abuse of commemo-rative festivals is an opportunity for the abuse of memory. There is, however, an ethics of memory precisely in the good use of commemora-tive acts against the ritualised commemoration.'[35] One repetition seeks to sustain a dominance based on the recurrence of the triumphal and antagonistic, the other is the reactivation of the untimely, that rupture in the social fabric articulated by a people-yet-to-come that we have argued in the first chapter was one characteristic of the civil rights movement. Deleuze writes of this function in his book *Difference and Repetition*:

> To repeat is to behave in a certain manner, but in relation to some-thing unique or singular which has no equal or equivalent. And perhaps this repetition at the level of external conduct echoes, for its own part, a more secret vibration which animates it, a more pro-found, internal repetition within the singular. This is the apparent paradox of festivals: they repeat an 'unrepeatable'. They do not add a second and a third time to the first, but carry the first time to the 'nth' power. With respect to this power, repetition interiorizes and thereby reverses itself: as Péguy says, it is not Federation Day which commemorates or represents the fall of the Bastille, but the fall of the Bastille which celebrates and repeats in advance all the Federa-tion days, or Monet's first water lily which repeats all the others.[36]

One type of repetition at work in Northern Ireland is orientated towards the idea of an origin, fixed and eternal, which is forcibly represented in something like the loyalist performance; the other is defined to a much greater degree by a notion of a simulacrum where the iterability of the subject is defined by the singular and the contingent. The visible disintegration of Cooper on screen seems to give shape to this process of tenuous subjectivity. Both films, in the different ways outlined, function as acts of certain kinds of repetition, both seek to take possession of the past and mobilise it to intervene in the present, to unblock the moment of time frozen during that brief period in Derry.

5

If We Dead Awakened
Thomas Kinsella's
Butcher's Dozen

It is possible that there is no other memory than the memory of wounds.[1]

. . . *even the dead* will not be safe from the enemy if he wins.[2]

On a large-screen television in one of the beautifully-lit rooms of the Museum of Free Derry in Glenfada Park, the images and sounds of Bloody Sunday are replayed several times a day. As you move around the small museum, past the Warholesque images of the faces of the dead men, and the fourteen wooden crosses that are carried as part of the annual commemoration events to the Bloody Sunday Memorial in Joseph Place, and the commemorative posters, and the display cabinets containing childhood and family photographs of the dead, the sounds of Bloody Sunday accompany you. The effect is immersive, and this is, of course, a well-established device of the modern museum. The act of looking at objects (modest things made strange and poignant by their incongruity – snapshots, bullet casings, *In Memoriam* cards) is only part of the experience of experiencing the museum's version of Bloody Sunday. The visitor's gaze is supplemented by a powerful aural influence in which the singing, the shouting, the shooting and the screaming captured on television news footage of the afternoon of 30 January 1972 provide a soundtrack to any visit to this remarkable place.

Above the noises of that afternoon a poem recited by three voices – one female, two male – seems to provide a commentary of sorts on the scenes you are watching or hearing. Depending upon what point you pick up or become aware of, the narrative, the voices are despairing, furious, accusatory, bullish, defeated, argumentative, analytical, polemical, humorous, ameliorative. The poem is Thomas Kinsella's *Butcher's Dozen* and its place and its function here in the heart of the Bogside, here in the museum that 'tells the story' not only of the day itself, but also its immediate contexts and aftermaths (the Civil Rights Campaign, the existence of Free Derry, internment without trial, Operation Motorman), is extraordinarily apt. Like the objects in the display

Figure 9.   Crosses at the Bloody Sunday monument, Joseph Place, Bogside *(Photo courtesy Tom Herron)*

cabinets, Kinsella's poem is a minor thing that has somehow persisted over many years as both a statement of problematic witness and as an act of ethical opposition to the state-sanctioned and state-endorsed official truth of Bloody Sunday. It is a remarkable poem, not just for the fact that, at least in formal terms, it is so unlike anything the poet had undertaken before, but also for its political boldness, for its discursive timeliness, for its refusal of the state's attempt to impose a legal and discursive hegemony, and for the brilliance with which it attempts (problematically, as we will see) to listen to the voices of the Bloody Sunday dead.

Butcher's Dozen is not the only poem written in response to Bloody Sunday and its aftermath. Seamus Heaney wrote a ballad ('The Road to Derry') soon after the killings,[3] and he incorporated the unforgettable images of the funerals of Wednesday 2 February 1972 into his poem 'Casualty' (1979):

> PARAS THIRTEEN, the walls said,
> BOGSIDE NIL. That Wednesday
> Everybody held
> His breath and trembled.
>
> .   .   .
>
> It was a day of cold
> Raw silence, wind-blown
> Surplice and soutane:
> Rained-on, flower-laden
> Coffin after coffin
> Seemed to float from the door
> Of the packed cathedral
> Like blossoms on slow water.
> The common funeral
> Unrolled its swaddling band,
> Lapping, tightening
> Till we were braced and bound
> Like brothers in a ring.[4]

The news of what had happened in the Bogside on 30 January prompted immediate responses by several poets and songwriters: Seamus Deane's 'After Derry, 30 January 1972' was written in the days following the killings; John Lennon and Yoko Ono's furious 'Sunday Bloody Sunday' was written and recorded in New York in February 1972; and Thomas McCarthy's 'Counting the Dead on the Radio' was produced several weeks later. Local people, too, produced numerous poems recording disbelief and anger at what had happened. But among all the poetry and song lyrics produced in the immediate aftermath of the killings and in later years (most notable among these later representations are U2's

'Sunday Bloody Sunday'[5] [1984], Christy Moore's 'Minds Locked Shut' [1996] and Sharon Meenan and Killian Mullan's 'I Wasn't Even Born' [1997]), Kinsella's poem stands apart as the most provocative and complex response to Bloody Sunday and its narrativisation in the Widgery Report, and it is for this reason that we give it such prominence in this chapter.

Over the course of the evening of 30 January the radio and television news reports were constantly updated to include the latest number of victims. Kinsella was at home in Dublin when RTÉ radio issued news reports of the killings. He recounts how 'the BBC in London announced that gunmen had opened fire on the army and that bombers in the crowd had forced the troops to retaliate; there was a lot of specific detail, supplied by the army'.[6] Several days later he travelled north to visit the Bogside and to attend the following weekend's NICRA rally in Newry. His walk through the Bogside provides, as we shall see, the dramatic conceit for his poem's speaker's encounter with the ghosts of the dead men. But it was less the killings themselves, and more the version of those killings set out in the Widgery Report, that prompted the poems:

> In Lord Widgery's cold putting aside of truth, the nth in a historical series of expedient falsehoods – with Injustice literally wigged out as Justice – it was evident to me that we were suddenly very close to the operations of the evil real causes.[7]

Having read the Irish newspapers' detailed reports of the evidence presented to the tribunal, Kinsella records his shock at how little relation the final report had to the weight of evidence that had 'accumulated into a clear indictment of the British troops and their officers'.[8] It was not the scope or the procedures of the tribunal that sparked the poem (indeed the poem takes the form of a quasi-tribunal and adheres tenaciously to the principles of law and justice) but the incongruity between the evidence presented to it and the Lord Chief Justice's interpretation of that evidence. From its opening lines through to the concluding vision, the poem is anchored in a belief in the necessity for due legal process, for fairness, for justice, and finally, for truth. And so, in a context where official truth had been established via the most callous misreading of the evidence, and in which voices of opposition were literally written out of this official account of events, Kinsella set to work.

With astonishing speed, the poem 'was finished, printed and published within a week of the publication of the Widgery Report'.[9] Produced 'in large quantities as a cheap pamphlet' and bearing on its front cover the design of the badge issued at the 6 February march and rally at Newry (a black coffin with the number 13 superimposed upon it), *Butcher's Dozen* appeared in shops all over Dublin at the price, as the back cover tells us, of Ten Pence. Although it is hard to gauge the visibility outside Dublin of this almost impossibly-thin, buff-coloured pamphlet, it was reprinted over the following weeks in several Irish newspapers and magazines, prompting considerable comment, some of it scathing (most notably James Simmons's absurd attack and parody in *Fortnight*) and some of it prescient, such as that of an anonymous reviewer in *Civil Rights*, the newsletter of NICRA, who predicted that Kinsella's 'account of the Derry Massacre will long outlive British Propaganda efforts to cover up the murder of civil rights marchers'.[10] Gerald Dawe's recollection of reading the poem when it first appeared captures something of the poem's contemporary impact:

> It was with a sense of outrage and disgust that the people read the Widgery Report. It had turned reality inside-out by making the unarmed marchers into a guerrilla force and the Paratroopers into a restrained and disciplined army. *Butcher's Dozen*, which was handed round in its frail pamphlet form, summed up that nightmarish world . . . the ballad cauterised the wound.[11]

The public nature of the poem was fortified the following year when, during the first-anniversary commemorations in Derry, it was read in its entirety by Vanessa Redgrave at the site of the proposed Bloody Sunday memorial. Although the poem has not featured in subsequent commemorative events, its presence as a soundtrack to any visit to the Museum of Free Derry, its inclusion on a commemorative poster and, perhaps more importantly, its own acute sense of injustice, ensures its centrality to the campaign for justice.

As a public poem *Butcher's Dozen* joins a canon shaped by other twentieth-century public/political poems, such as W. H. Auden's 'Spain 1937', W. B. Yeats's 'Easter 1916', Robert Lowell's 'Waking Early Sunday Morning' (1965) and Tony Harrison's *v.* (1985) and 'The Gaze of the Gorgon' (1992). And there is of course a much longer and broader tradition of political (if not necessarily public) poetry that encompasses such figures as Milton, Dryden, Blake, Wordsworth, Shelley, Burns, Mandelstam, Brecht, MacDiarmid, Neruda, Herbert, Ratushinskaya and others. 'Almost invariably', Tom Paulin argues,

> a political poem is a public poem, and it often begins in a direct response to a current event, just as a pamphlet or a piece of journalism springs from and addresses a particular historical moment.[12]

Born as it is from a moment of emergency, the language and the form of the public poem are, also invariably, impure, tending towards the mnemonics of the ballad or rhyming couplets, to insistent and at times forced rhythm, to declaration rather than introspection; to doggerel, in fact. Writing on *Butcher's Dozen* seven years after its initial publication, Kinsella sees the poem as a form of *bricolage* appropriate to, and partaking of, its moment of production:

> The pressures were special, the insult strongly felt, and the timing vital if the response was to matter, in all its kinetic impurity. Reaching for the nearest aid, I found the *aisling* form – that never quite extinct Irish political verse-form – in a late parodied guise: in the coarse energies and nightmare Tribunal of Merriman's *Midnight Court*. One changed one's standards, chose the doggerel route, and charged . . .[13]

That final phrase brings us close to the retaliatory energy of *Butcher's Dozen*, and brings us close, quite frankly, to its poetic and its political design. This was never going to be a lament or an elegy for the dead; it was an accusation, an urgent demand, an attack. It was 'written in rage and haste' and it exhibits, unsurprisingly in the circumstances, all the features of the impure and indecorous public poem. And while some of the best-known public poems in English were written in response to, and condemnation of, particular events – the Peterloo Massacre (Shelley), the execution of the leaders of the 1916 Rising (Yeats), the decimation of the British coal-mining industry (Harrison) – there is often a considerable delay between the moment of writing and the date of publication. For example, it took Yeats over four years to publish 'Easter 1916'[14] and many more years for Leigh Hunt to publish Shelley's *The Masque of Anarchy* (a key intertext of *Butcher's Dozen*). And while there are often good reasons for these delays, the very belatedness of the poem lets the moment of its conception pass; by the time it appears, the enemy has moved on and official forgetting has neutralised the anger (if not the trauma) out of which the poem sprang in the first place.

Kinsella's poem is different. Its date of publication (26 April 1972), its form (the pamphlet), its nominal cost and its undisguised concern with the present moment (a moment in which a veil was being drawn over truth and justice) make it an explicit intervention in the circumstances immediately following Bloody Sunday and its caricature in Widgery. The outrage of the poem comes, furthermore, from Kinsella's sense that this most recent 'grotesque mockery of justice'[15] is only the latest episode in a long-standing series of such denials. So, while the poem is set in the Bogside of early 1972, a broader historical–political awareness is at work. This is perhaps the reason why, of all the poems written in response to Bloody Sunday, it is Kinsella's poem that has attracted most criticism and has remained the most sustained poetic treatment of the day. Rather than merely lamenting the deaths of that day (not that there is anything ignoble in that), Kinsella shares the type of contextual reading of Bloody Sunday articulated by Seamus Deane:

Since the time of Parnell, through 1916, 1918–22, and 1969 to the present day, the same policy has been in place: when Irish protest became emphatic, it was criminalised. Then the law was used to justify both that policy of criminalisation and the killings of anyone who came from the community that had been so cleverly and outrageously misrepresented.[16]

Butcher's Dozen is both testament to a gross misrepresentation and an attempt to re-present, albeit in a form of ghostly and abject witness, the truth of what befell the dead, injured and traumatised of that day.

An *aisling* in the Bogside

In acknowledging his debt to Brian Merriman's *The Midnight Court* Kinsella sets his own poem squarely within the tradition of Irish *aisling* poetry. Associated primarily with eighteenth-century political poetry, the *aisling* (dream or vision poem) is the poetic form *par excellence* of the native dispossessed. Originating as a form of love poetry from perhaps as early as the seventh century, and having secondary roots in that tradition of medieval Western European poetry of the parliament or the court of love,[17] the *aisling* provides a glimpse of a utopia in the form of a dream that is then immediately undercut as the dreamer awakes to the harsh material and political realities of the existing order. The form, especially in the work of Aogán Ó Rathaille and Eoghan Rua Ó Súilleabháin, conjoins the political and the amatory in that the object of the vision, the beautiful sky-woman, or *spéirbhean,* announces to the dreamer the coming of Stuart deliverance from the hardships of the Penal Laws enacted after the Williamite Wars. The final stanza of Ó Súilleabháin's 'Ceo Draíochta'/'A Magic Mist' is exemplary:

> If our Stuart returned o'er the ocean
> to the lands of Inis Áilge in full course
> with a fleet of Louis' men, and the Spaniard's,
> by dint of joy truly I'd be
> on a prancing white steed of swift mettle
> ever sluicing them out with much shot
> – after which I'd not injure my spirit
> standing guard for the rest of my life.[18]

Seamus Deane characterises the *aisling* as 'less an expression of an unrealistic hope than it is an expression of a permanently rebellious attitude towards the existing order'.[19] Yet, it is striking that Kinsella does not himself cite the millenarian visions of Ó Rathaille's famous 'Gile na Gile'/'Brightness Most Bright', nor even Art Mac Cumhaigh's bleak 'Úr-Chill an Chreagáin'/'The Churchyard of Creagán', in which any hope of

Jacobite deliverance has vanished, but the later parody of the genre in the shape of Merriman's thousand-line poem, *Cúirt an Mheán Oíche/The Midnight Court*. This, on the face of it, seems an odd choice of model, given that Merriman's poem is, as Ó Tuama puts it, 'certainly the greatest comic poem ever written in Ireland . . . full of tumultuous bouts of great good humour, verbal dexterity and Rabelaisian ribaldry'.[20] Through all its translations (but particularly in Frank O'Connor's unabashedly censor-baiting version of 1945) it is the rough humour and frank sexuality that marks the poem out from its more sedate contemporaries. Here is a section from Heaney's translation of a passage when a young woman complains about the sexual ineptitude of Irish men:

> I'm scorched and tossed, a sorry case
> Of nerves and drives and neediness,
> Depressed, obsessed, awake at night,
> Unused, unsoothed, disconsolate,
> A throbbing ache, a dumb discord,
> My mind and bed like a kneading board.
> O Warden of the Crag, incline!
> Observe the plight of Ireland's women,
> For if things go on like this, then fuck it!
> The men will have to be abducted![21]

And here, in Ciarán Carson's translation, is the 'dirty old josser's' reply to the woman:

> Here's Sheila the Gig in the latest of fashion!
> No wonder you're single, you grubby wee ticket,
> Your clan had not even the spunk to be wicked!
> Whingers and wastrels, the whole bloody lot,
> What little they had has long gone to pot!
> That father of yours was a classical case
> Of a freeloading bum . . .[22]

So, why *The Midnight Court* as a model? Why, in a poem so concerned with the legal whitewashing of state-sanctioned murder, does Kinsella turn to a comic eighteenth-century Irish poem obsessed with sex?

The most obvious reason is that *The Midnight Court* is itself a poem of tribunal. Its setting is a people's court, a midnight gathering of women who arraign the poet and all Irish men on charges, as Heaney delicately puts it, of 'insufficient amorous drive and a failure of conjugal will'.[23] Merriman's experiment with, and expansion of, the *aisling* form encourages multiple perspectives on the central issue concerning the 'court': namely, the desperate state of Irish manhood. This is not a typical *aisling* in which a beautiful *sidh* or *spéirbhean* (as embodiment of

Éire) voices noble aspirations for Stuart delivery; nor is it a court of law, with its strict protocols and rules on admissible and inadmissible evidence. It is, rather, a eutopian place, a kind of proto-Habermasian 'ideal speech situation', in which discordant statements, insults and replies are traded. Everyone is allowed to speak in whatever form of language they choose, and all is carried on in a colourfully confrontational communicative space. It is, as Heaney points out, 'special not only because it is a woman's court, but also because it is fair and just and incorruptible, a dream court which momentarily redresses the actual penal system under which the native population have to endure'.[24]

Immediately we begin to see resonances in Kinsella's 230-line poem. *Butcher's Dozen* begins where British law has so peremptorily finished. After Widgery there would be no troubling of the official version of the events of 30 January 1972. The authority of law is such that Lord Widgery's eleven conclusions remain *until this day* the official truth of Bloody Sunday, their patent absurdity notwithstanding. But much in the same way as Shelley inverts divine order, so that the English king himself becomes the figure of anarchy, so now the assembled ghosts of the Bloody Sunday dead turn their gaze upon the British state (and its legal, military and political apparatuses) and accuse *it* of perpetrating injustice. What sets itself up as justice is revealed by its victims to be the opposite. *Butcher's Dozen* is not exactly the type of people's tribunal that was actually considered as an option by campaigners,[25] in that there is no opportunity for the soldiers or the politicians to give their points of view. However, it is a form of spectral burlesque in which the thirteen dead men return to give 'voice' to the truth that had been so clumsily edited out of Lord Widgery's report and conclusions. In listening to the 'voices' of the dead, Kinsella is in fact listening to those other voices of the living witnesses whose evidence to the tribunal was either ignored completely or deliberately misread and then misrepresented. In doing so, Kinsella both refuses the state's self-declared prerogative to have the final say on the matter, and simultaneously keeps faith in a system that should have – at its core – a fundamental and irreducible epistemological and juridical function. That Lord Widgery's report has flouted the truth presented in evidence is the single most important catalyst for Kinsella's poem of 'momentary redress', with its overriding concern, announced in its opening lines, for truth:

> I went with Anger at my heel
> Through Bogside of the bitter zeal
> – Jesus pity! – on a day
> Of cold and drizzle and decay.
> A month had passed. Yet there remained
> A murder smell that stung and stained.
> On flats and alleys – over all –
> It hung; on battered roof and wall,

> On wreck and rubbish scattered thick,
> On sullen steps and pitted brick.
> And where I came where thirteen died
> It shrivelled up my heart. I sighed
> And looked about that brutal place
> Of rage and terror and disgrace.[26]

Amongst the Augustan personification, the rhyming couplets, the pathetic fallacies, and the dramatic caesurae, Kinsella deploys the strange phrase 'bitter zeal'. In so doing he follows St James, who, in his epistle, cautions against acts, thoughts and utterances that might displease the Lord: 'But if you have bitter zeal, and there be contention in your hearts: glory not and be not liars against the truth.'[27] 'Bitter zeal' is the absence of truth as an embodiment of heavenly wisdom. Bitter zeal is 'not wisdom, descending from above but earthly, sensual, devilish'. By placing the phrase – that has no other precedents other than its use in James's epistle – in the opening moment of a poem written as a 'Lesson for the Octave of Widgery',[28] Kinsella establishes his overarching concern: how, in the face of evil dressed up as Justice and Truth, are goodness, justice and truth to find a voice, to, 'hold a plea'?[29]

It will already be clear that Merriman's *Court* also provides for Kinsella the major conceit for his poem: the encounter and converse with ghosts. *The Midnight Court* is, as Ciarán Carson points out, suffused with spectrality. In a close reading of the single word *aerach* at the end of a couplet in the final part of the poem, Carson reveals the ghostliness operating at every level of the text:

> The words, the more that you look at them, become foreign, eerie and strange: and *aerach* also means 'haunted' or 'weird'. Dinneen has the expression *áit aerach*, 'a lonely place, a place haunted by ghosts', which is the landscape in which the poem itself is set; and then we realise that the first word in the couplet, *taibhseach*, does indeed mean 'spirited'; but it also means 'ghostly'. For the protagonists of the 'Court', including 'Merriman' himself, are ghosts, summoned into being by language.[30]

Butcher's Dozen, too, is set in a tightly bounded space haunted by ghosts. For the most part the poem is made up of the 'voices' of those ghosts, many of them corresponding at times closely, at other times more tangentially (especially as the poem progresses, and as we move from testimony to condemnation), with the dead of Bloody Sunday. For example, the first voice to answer the poet seems to evoke Jackie Duddy, the first person to be shot dead on the day. Jackie was shot in the back while running away from the advancing paratroopers, and his ghost's words present the reaction of the soldiers as entirely excessive:

> Once there lived a hooligan.
> A pig came up, and away he ran.
> Here lies one in blood and bones,
> Who lost his life for throwing stones.

Moments later we hear a chorus of voices as the ghosts of the men shot at the rubble barricade on Rossville Street appear to the poet:

> More voices rose. I turned and saw
> Three corpses forming, red and raw,
> From dirt and stone. Each upturned face
> Stared unseeing from its place:
> 'Behind this barrier, blighters three,[31]
> We scrambled back and made to flee.
> The guns cried *Stop*, and here lie we.'

The next identifiable voice is that of the ghost of Gerald Donaghy, who, in the minutes after (or even before) his death in the back of a Ford Cortina at an army checkpoint, seems to have been subject to an evidence-planting operation.[32] Ventriloquising the conclusions of the tribunal (a strange anachronism here: how, shot dead as he was on the 30 January, can the ghost be in a position to know, and then incorporate into his own speech, Widgery's traducement, which was, of course, published eleven weeks later?), this is what the ghost says about what happens to Donaghy after his death:

> 'A bomber I. I travelled light
> – Four pounds of nails and gelignite
> About my person, hid so well
> They seemed to vanish where I fell.
> When the bullet stopped my breath
> A doctor sought the cause of death.
> He upped my shirt, undid my fly,
> Twice he moved my limbs awry,
> And noticed nothing. By and by
> A soldier, with his sharper eye,
> Beheld the four elusive rockets
> Stuffed in my coat and trouser pockets.
> Yes, they must be strict with us,
> Even in death so treacherous!'

Although Widgery describes the circumstances of what may have happened to Donaghy's body as 'relatively unimportant', he expends considerable effort in privileging the demonstrably unreliable evidence of the soldiers over the detailed and numerous submissions of civilian eyewitnesses, not one of whom detected the said bombs anywhere about his person.[33] Despite the weight of evidence presented to the tribunal giving credence to the suspicion that the nail bombs had been planted on Donaghy's body by person or persons unknown, this is how Widgery, in a bewildering passage of bad reasoning, shapes an acceptable truth out of the dark materials presented to him in evidence:

> After Donaghy fell he was taken into the house of Mr Raymond Rogan at 10 Abbey Park. He had been shot in the abdomen. He was wearing a blue denim blouse and trousers with pockets of the kind that open to the front rather than to the side. The evidence was that some at least of his pockets were examined for evidence of his identity and that his body was examined by Dr Kevin Swords, who normally worked in a hospital in Lincoln. Dr Swords' opinion was that Donaghy was alive but should go to hospital immediately. Mr Rogan volunteered to drive him there in his car. Mr Leo Young went with him to help. The car was stopped at a military check-point in Barrack Street, where Mr Rogan and Mr Young were made to get out. The car was then driven by a soldier to the Regimental Aid Post of 1st Battalion Royal Anglian Regiment, where Donaghy was examined by the Medical Officer (Soldier 138) who pronounced him dead. The Medical Officer made a more detailed examination shortly afterwards but on neither occasion did he notice anything unusual in Donaghy's pockets. After another short interval, and whilst Donaghy's body still lay on the back seat of Mr Rogan's car, it was noticed that he had a nail bomb in one of his trouser pockets (as photographed in RUC photographs EP 5A/26 and 27). An Ammunition Technical Officer (Bomb Disposal Officer, Soldier 127) was sent for and found four nail bombs in Donaghy's pockets.
>
> There are two possible explanations of this evidence. First, that the bombs had been in Donaghy's pockets throughout and had passed unnoticed by the Royal Anglians' Medical Officer, Dr Swords, and others who had examined the body; secondly that the bombs had been deliberately planted on the body by some unknown person after the Medical Officer's examination. These possibilities were exhaustively examined in evidence because, although the matter is a relatively unimportant detail of the events of the afternoon, it is no doubt of great concern to Donaghy's family. I think that on a balance of probabilities the bombs were in Donaghy's pockets throughout. His jacket and trousers were not removed but were merely opened as he lay on his back in the car. It seems likely that these relatively bulky objects would have been noticed when Donaghy's body was examined; but it is conceivable that they were not and the alternative explanation of a plant is mere speculation. No evidence was offered as to where the bombs might have come from, who might have placed them or why Donaghy should have been singled out for this treatment.[34]

After the ghost of Gerald Donaghy has spoken in the poem, the shades of Michael McDaid, John Young and Willie Nash appear.

Speaking in chorus, these ghosts attest to one of the most shameful episodes of that shameful day – when the injured were loaded into a Pig and were left, according to several eyewitness reports, to die on its metal floor:[35]

> 'We three met close when we were dead.
> Into an armoured car they piled us
> Where our mingled blood defiled us,
> Certain, if not dead before,
> To suffocate upon the floor.
> Careful bullets in the back
> Stopped our terrorist attack,
> And so three dangerous lives are done –
> Judged, condemned and shamed in one.'

After these ghosts have had their say, the spectral voices of the poem become less personal, less easy to identify as relating directly to any of the dead men, as they turn their attention initially to the Widgery inquiry and then to the broader effects of British imperialism in Ireland. It is an extraordinary sequence in which the dead of Bloody Sunday, not content to remain dead, return as spectres to argue their cases and causes. And this is no small or easy matter for them: it is a struggle for them to speak through their pain. Constantly we are reminded that in 'coming back' to give voice they also return to the moment of their death, with all the distress that that entails. As the ghosts speak we, too, are drawn to the very spot at which they died. As the poet wanders around the killing field of the Bogside we, like him, are forced to register the circumstances in which the men became ghosts. And while Edna Longley is partly correct in feeling that 'the ghoulish way in which the dead are introduced . . . destroys their dignity',[36] she underplays the heroic nature of their revenance: in assuming ghostly form in order that their voices be heard, the dead men pay a high price, in that they must return pathetically and uncannily to the moment of their 'becoming-dead':

> There in a ghostly pool of blood
> A crumpled phantom hugged the mud
>
> . . .
>
> I turned and saw
> Three corpses forming, red and raw,
> From dirt and stone. Each upturned face
> Stared unseeing from its place
>
> . . .
>
> Then from left and right they came,
> More mangled corpses, bleeding, lame,
> Holding their wounds.
>
> . . .

> He capered weakly, racked with pain,
> His dead hair plastered in the rain.

Dead and disgraced though they are, the ghosts have little time for self-pity: their focus is on Widgery and the system he represents. One asks, 'Does it need recourse to law/To tell ten thousand what they saw?' and follows up with a more pointed attack on Widgery's interpretation of the evidence:

> 'The news is out. The troops were kind.
> Impartial justice has to find
> We'd be alive and well today
> If we had let them have their way.
> Yet England, even as you lie,
> You give the facts that you deny.'

Another 'joking spectre', deploying language reminiscent of *Macbeth*, sees the massacre as a sort of grotesque concoction made from the detritus of a history of colonialism:

> 'Take a bunch of stunted shoots,
> A tangle of transplanted roots,
> Ropes and rifles, feathered nests,
> Some dried colonial interests,
> A hard unnatural union grown
> In a bed of blood and bone,
> Tongue of serpent, gut of hog
> Spiced with spleen of underdog.
> Stir in, with oaths of loyalty,
> Sectarian supremacy,
> And heat, to make a proper broth,
> In a bouillon of bitter Scotch.
> Last, the choice ingredient: you.
> Now, to crown your Irish stew,
> Boil it over, make a mess.
> A most imperial success!'

Another spectre foretells, with foresight that is startlingly uncanny in the circumstances, the death of non-violent forms of civil rights protest in the face of colonial brutality:

> Simple lessons cut most deep.
> This lesson in our hearts we keep:
> Persuasion, protest, arguments,
> The milder forms of violence,
> Earn nothing but polite neglect.

England, the way to your respect
Is via murderous force, it seems;
You push us to your own extremes.

Once this spectre gets going there appears to be little to stop him, as he progresses deftly through images and emblems of the Northern Ireland colony. Pausing only to clear his throat from the 'bloody sputum' that impedes his speech, he finishes 'with his eyes a-glow:/'You came, you saw, you conquered.' He is ultimately brought to a halt by the final spectre, who interrupts his tirade with the stark simplicity of 'Yet pity is akin to love':[37]

The thirteenth corpse beside him said,
Smiling in its bloody head,
'And though there's reason for alarm
In dourness and a lack of charm
Their cursed plight calls out for patience.
They, even they, with other nations
Have a place, if we can find it.
Love our changeling! Guard and mind it.
Doomed from birth, a cursed heir,
Theirs is the hardest lot to bear,
Yet not impossible, I swear,
If England would but clear the air
And brood at home on her disgrace –
Everything to its own place.
Face their walls of dole and fear
And be of reasonable cheer.'

For a recently-ghosted victim of state-sanctioned murder this is, of course, an extraordinarily conciliatory statement. More than this, it articulates an amazing capacity for forgiveness without condition; a proper forgiveness, which Jacques Derrida considers 'should not be . . . normal, normative, normalizing. It *should* remain exceptional and extraordinary, in the face of the impossible'.[38] While it might be tempting to consider this as the poem's final or summative vision, this would be to do an injustice to the sentiments and the anger and, indeed, the arguments of the other ghosts. Because, while *Butcher's Dozen* is, indeed, a convocation of spectres, the 'voices' of the ghosts are clearly and carefully differentiated. In marked contrast to the Lord Chief Justice's single narrative, in which differences between the victims are blatantly erased – the most egregious example is the way in which, despite plentiful eyewitness evidence detailing the specifics of each killing, Widgery amalgamates into a single occurrence the deaths of Jim Wray, Gerald McKinney, Gerald Donaghy and William McKinney[39] – Kinsella insists upon heteroglossia, upon a diverse dialogism between the ghosts themselves, and between them and the poem's narrator. Just like the dead of Friel's *The Freedom of the City* there are huge variations in the levels of political motivation between the ghosts. And this, in fact, articulates rather accurately the very real differences between the dead men, some of whom were actively involved in civil rights protest, while others were entirely uninvolved (and in some cases wholly uninterested in) politics, republican or otherwise.[40] Merriman's *aisling* provides, again, the model for such dialogism. More than other influences – such as Swift's 'Ireland' and Shelley's 'Masque of Anarchy', both of which present powerful but entirely monologic voices of condemnation – it is the multiplicity of voices within *The Midnight Court* that proves so attractive to Kinsella. *Butcher's Dozen* as heteroglossia retains an ethical affiliation to the memory of the dead men and marks itself out as an unsettling, oppositional performance in relation, not only to Widgery's monologism, but also to the political imperatives of the state that sanctioned and so readily endorsed the rigidities of both his processes and his 'findings'.

As a modern-day *aisling*, *Butcher's Dozen* returns to the material conditions of post-Bloody Sunday, post-Widgery Derry with devastating effect. Having had their say, the ghosts return to the 'galleried-earth', leaving the poet stranded in the very centre of 'that brutal place':

> I stood like a ghost. My fingers strayed
> Along the fatal barricade.
> The gentle rainfall drifting down
> Over Colmcille's town
> Could not refresh, only distil
> In silent grief from hill to hill.

In her fine analysis of the poem and its critical reception, Derval Tubridy detects, in these final lines, a shift of focus. The poem, according to Tubridy, turns 'to the earth, which is both a common denominator and a divider, and looks back to a time before sectarian division'.[41] We are not entirely convinced. Kinsella (or the poem's speaker) stands bereft, speechless, both ghostly and ghosted: he has had a visitation from these revenants, but any sense of optimism suggested by the final ghost's inclusive vision ('We all are what we are, and that/Is mongrel pure') is balanced by the closing image of the poet/speaker standing by the fatal (and pathetically ineffectual) barricade. The official silencing has not been breached. Let us not forget that the whole of *Butcher's Dozen* takes place in silence: these ghosts, like all ghosts, cannot produce voice; there is no *body* there to produce or sustain sound, and their painful performances have been observed only by the poet.[42] Even less substantially than this (some critics of the poem have argued), the spectres didn't appear at all; there was no apparition, less still a ghostly colloquy. The entire thing, they argue, is simply an act of ventriloquism by a poet falling prey to the temptation of propagandising. With honourable exceptions, almost all critical discussions of the poem assume that it is Kinsella speaking throughout, speaking through the voice of the narrator and imposing his voice upon the 'ghosts'.

We would refute any such readings that underestimate both the ethical concerns and the imaginative resources of Kinsella's poem. Where most critics prefer to see *Butcher's Dozen* as an act of ventriloquism, we prefer to see it as a strange but ultimately sympathetic communication with the Bloody Sunday dead. Of course, we will never know what the men felt about the circumstances of their death, and we will never know, because they did not have the opportunity to comment upon the ways in which they were traduced in Lord Widgery's report. But *Butcher's Dozen* is an attempt to cross the border between life and death, between what is known and unknown. It operates in a spectral space – neither in the here nor the there – in the realm, as Derrida theorises it, of ghostly traces, cinders, impressions. Kinsella's poem pushes against the limits of the knowable by listening out for the traces of the dead. It is a risky business and it is of course vulnerable to the overdetermining will of the poet, who wishes to manipulate his ghosts for his own particular artistic and/or propagandist purposes: this was clearly the concern of several of the poem's critics. But we prefer to give Kinsella the benefit of the doubt. His urge to listen to and speak with the dead is similar to the desire expressed by Stephen Greenblatt, who, in the famous opening lines of his *Shakespearian Negotiations*, writes

> I began with the desire to speak with the dead . . . If I never believed that the dead could hear me, and if I knew that the dead could not speak, I was nonetheless certain that I could re-create a conversation with them. Even when I came to understand that in my most intense moments of straining to listen all I could hear was my own voice, even then I did not abandon my desire. It was true that I could hear only my own voice, but my own voice was also the voice of the dead, for the dead had contrived to leave textual traces of themselves, and those traces make themselves heard in the voices of the living.[43]

It is through the voices of the living that Kinsella 'accesses' the words of the dead. But for all the risks that this procedure may involve, we believe that the revised historical record of the events of the day will (most probably) bear out Kinsella's conviction that, just in the same way as the truth of Bloody Sunday was most indelibly inscribed upon the dead, so too is it in the 'voices' of the dead that the truth of Bloody Sunday will be found.

6

Casualties of Language
Brian Friel's *The Freedom of the City* and Frank McGuinness's *Carthaginians*

Those who live under the law are civilians; those who live beyond it are barbarians.[1]

When life is over we are taught to live.[2]

We suggested in Chapter 4 that Greengrass and McGovern are wedded, albeit in different ways and to varying degrees, to a theory of representation that would have us believe that their films are – by means of meticulous research, hypersensitive attention to authentic period and local details, deployment of the techniques of *cinéma vérité*, community involvement and, perhaps most importantly, an unwavering commitment to the belief in film's ability to somehow narrativise the *story* of Bloody Sunday – reconstructions of the 'real'. Nowhere in *Sunday* or *Bloody Sunday* is cognisance given to the fact that what the filmmakers have done is to produce yet another construction, yet another version, of what is supposed to have happened on the day. Both films seem immensely secure in their own procedures for producing authenticity and truth: 'This film is based on true events' states the closing epigraph of *Bloody Sunday*; 'this drama is based entirely on fact' state the opening credits of *Sunday*. This, perhaps generic, confidence is all the more apparent if we compare their productions to the work of playwrights who have responded (again in various degrees of representational felicity) to the events of 30 January 1972. At every level it is striking to see just how difficult the relationship between theatre and real-world is for playwrights who eschew conventions of realism when 'responding to' an event that was most definitely real, that was the result of real (political, military) motivations and actions and resulted in real effects (injury, death, the forsaking of civil means of social change in Northern Ireland in favour of physical force). Two of Ireland's foremost playwrights – Brian Friel and Frank McGuinness, both of whom have strong links to the city of Derry – have produced substantial pieces in response to Bloody Sunday. But, even that phrase, 'in response to', might suggest a rather too secure correspondence between the real and the imagined. Friel is at pains to dissociate his play, *The Freedom of the City* (1973), from the circumstances of Bloody Sunday, and Frank McGuinness's rendering in *Carthaginians* (1988) of the long-term trauma inflicted by Bloody Sunday takes a considerable time to arrive at a point where Bloody Sunday and its victims are openly acknowledged by his characters, even though their impact seems to haunt every moment of the play's action. Neither play attempts to be a faithful rendering of either the established or the contested 'events' of Bloody Sunday. More problematic than this, they both contain elements that would challenge established nationalist, or pro-civil rights, or Derry-centric versions of the day. There is a distinctly sceptical dimension to both that would render problematic any suggestion of them articulating a definable memory of (less still an interpretation of) Bloody Sunday.

Phantom scenario: *The Freedom of the City*

Had the Field Day Theatre Company been established in 1973 rather than 1980, it is likely that Brian Friel's *The Freedom of the City* would have premièred, as all Field Day productions did, in the very building in which the play's action is set. Watching the performance in the Great Hall of Derry's Guildhall, the audience would have been only too well aware that it was just along the corridor, in the Mayor's Parlour, where Lily, Michael and Skinner, the main characters of the piece, find themselves under siege by the British soldiers, and that it was just outside the building (on the steps leading down to Guildhall Square) where they are shot dead. And, of course, the events of the previous January that took place in the Bogside would inevitably have haunted every second of the play. How could they not have done, when Friel's drama follows the three civil rights protestors from the chaos of a proscribed march from the Creggan to a rally in Guildhall Square,[3] into the forbidden territory of the Mayor's Parlour, and then out into the army's line of fire? And how could Lord Widgery's systematic misreading of Bloody Sunday not have impinged upon a theatrical event that accumulates and then condenses into the 'official truth' multiple versions of what happened on that day to a point where the voices of the victims themselves are lost in the white noise of competing discourses (forensic, patriotic, journalistic, religious, sociological, and legal)? Most of all, how could the still-fresh memory of Bloody Sunday not have saturated this performance when the entire piece is shot through with replica images of the day: army vehicles advancing at speed towards protestors, a woman addressing a civil rights meeting that erupts in pandemonium as shooting begins, the attack on the crowd by the 1st Battalion Parachute Regiment (with reserve companies from the 1st Battalion King's Own Border Regiment and two companies of the 3rd Battalion Royal Regiment of Fusiliers in attendance – just as they had been on 30 January 1972)[4] and a priest bearing a white handkerchief as he kneels by the victims lying dead or dying on the rubble-strewn street?

This final image is in fact where the play begins: the opening scene presents the three protagonists lying dead in front of us on the stage. Because during the course of the play these dead come back to life, they are aware of the tribunal's verdict upon them (that they were armed terrorists) but they do not comment upon it: the play does nothing to disturb the silence that settled on the city of Derry in the wake of the killings. Indeed, the entire lack of response (be it shock, or grief, or rancour) is one of the most unsettling aspects of Friel's play. The final sounds we hear are the judge's words followed by the noise of automatic gunfire. Then there is utter and terminal silence. Here in the Guildhall, that most explicit symbol of the city's and the province's links with its imperial sponsors, is a play located at the exact moment when the inequalities built into the edifice of Northern Ireland were finally laid bare, and when, in an act of brutal and stupid repression, the statelet entered (though it was barely conceivable to any of the participants in the events of the period) 'the first phase of its long, slow disintegration'.[5] The effects of this phantom performance would, no doubt, have been devastating to a Derry audience in 1973, especially as the play offers absolutely no amelioration of the hurt that was inflicted on the day of the killings and then compounded by the official verdict of the generally honourable behaviour of the killers and the implied or actual culpability of those killed. Benjamin's dictum that '*even the dead will not be safe from the enemy if he wins*'[6] seems to be entirely borne out by Friel's drama.

As it was, the play opened in Dublin at the Abbey Theatre on 20 February 1973 and then at the Royal Court Theatre in London on 27 February 1973 in a separate production directed by Albert Finney. The reviews were muted, and many of the London reviewers were critical of what they saw as the play's alleged political bias. There were productions also in Chicago and in New York, where, after only nine performances, the production was quietly pulled. *The Freedom of the City* was revived in 2005 at the Finsborough Theatre, London, only a few months after Richard Norton-Taylor's *Bloody Sunday – Scenes from Saville* opened at the Tricycle Theatre in Kilburn. Both productions received overwhelmingly positive reviews.

From the time of writing, Brian Friel has voiced concerns about *The Freedom of the City*. Speaking to Eavan Boland in 1973 he states categorically that it 'is not a play about Bloody Sunday. In fact the play began long before Bloody Sunday happened. I was working on this theme for about ten months . . . and then Bloody Sunday happened, and the play I was writing, and wasn't succeeding with, suddenly found a focus.'[7] But even this sense of focus prompts a certain anxiety for the playwright:

> the play raises the old problem of writing about events which are still happening . . . The trouble about this particular play in many ways is that people are going to find something immediate in it, some kind of reportage. And I don't think that's in it at all. Very often an accident in history will bring about a meeting-point, a kind of fusion in you. And this is what happened. This is a play which is about poverty. But because we're all involved in the present situation people are going to say 'this is a very unfair play'. And of necessity it has got to be unfair in this public kind of way.[8]

Speaking to Fintan O'Toole in 1982, Friel continues to emphasise the difficulties he has with his own play:

> one of the problems with that play was that the experience of Bloody Sunday wasn't adequately distilled in me. I wrote it out of some kind of heat and some kind of immediate passion that I would want to have quieted a bit before I did it. It was really – do you remember that time? – it was a very emotive time. It was really a shattering experience that the British Army, this disciplined instrument, would go in as they did that time and shoot thirteen people. To be there on that occasion and – I didn't actually see people get shot – but, I mean, to have to throw yourself on the ground because people are firing at you is a very terrifying experience. Then the whole cover up afterwards was shattering too. I still had some kind of belief that the law is above reproach![9]

So here we have two authorial interpretations: the first firmly refuting any notion that the play 'is about' Bloody Sunday, while the second points to failings in the play due to the traumatic repercussions of Bloody Sunday and to the prematurity of the play itself. In fact, almost every feature of the play differs significantly from the most commonly accepted versions of that day. The action is set, not in the Bogside of January 1972, but in and around the Guildhall on a Saturday afternoon in February 1970. Three people are shot dead by the British Army on the day, not thirteen. And the circumstances of the final moments of the victims are quite distinct from those of the boys and men who were killed in Rossville Street, Joseph Place and Glenfada Court. Yes, the three are involved in a civil rights march, but the issue at hand is not internment, which would not be reintroduced in Northern Ireland until the following year. And so, immediately, a degree of caution is required if we are not to fall into the trap of simply regarding the play as either a faithful portrayal of 'real-life' events, or seeing it as an imaginative reworking of the day. Even though there are many elements that encourage a yoking of the play to the 'real' (most prominently, the language of the judge – who is 'English, in his early sixties' – often corresponds word-for-word with Lord Widgery's report), there is at the same time a patent effort on the part of the playwright to anachronise, to deterritorialise, to depart from the established or contested narratives of Bloody Sunday and thereby to render unstable any assumptions that the play will attempt to present the 'event' *as it really was*. At the same time, it is (we would argue) impossible to immunise a cultural product from the social and political processes surrounding it; so, while we acknowledge the author's forthright declaration, we do not necessarily accept it.

Why this distancing through anachronism? Why this deliberate confounding of representational felicity? Why might a play that so clearly invokes the killing and injuring of innocent people in the very place in which Friel spent his teenage and early adult years,[10] and at a protest march in which he himself participated, go to such lengths to dissociate itself from the specific circumstances of Bloody Sunday? While most of the play's critics are alert to the fact that *The Freedom of the City* is not straightforwardly 'about' Bloody Sunday (they tend to use phrases such as 'the play evokes the events of that day'), it is only through an act of epistemological repression, or through a determined forgetting, that the play's strange and uncanny commerce with the events of that day can be erased. This is a play that is not about Bloody Sunday, but yet Bloody Sunday inhabits it; as Pablo Picasso was reputed to have said following the liberation of Paris in 1944, 'I have not painted the war . . . but I have no doubt that the war is present in these paintings'.[11] What becomes clear in his interview with Boland is Friel's acute unease about the advisability or even the ability of (his) art to deal somehow with the here and the now: 'the trouble with Derry at the moment is that there is an articulation there, but it's a kind of clichéd articulation, because everybody is so obsessed with the media and what has happened yesterday that we have all got answers for everything'.[12] Living just outside Derry, but separated from both it and the rest of the North by the border, Friel needs to distance himself from those discourses that remain within the realm of fixed and stereotyped surety. The key question here, then, is how, or if, Friel escapes those nets to produce a narrative or a vision distinct from the clichéd truths circulating in Derry in the period immediately after Bloody Sunday.

By valorising the eye-witness testimony of his three imaginary characters over all other speech-acts that constitute the play, Friel places under severe interrogation the veridicity of all versions, all interpretations, of the meaning of their deaths and their participation in the civil rights protest. Every explanation of his main characters' behaviour – from the lies of the brigadier, to the distortions of the judge, to the sympathetic sociological analysis of Dr Dodds – is entirely impervious to the actions, thoughts and words of the three protagonists. The three are, in the fullest sense of the term, subaltern. We, the audience, observe them speaking to each other, but their speech remains unregarded and, as they are dead, unregardable by the powerful voices in the play. And consequently, they are incorporated without hesitation or discomfort into those other voices' versions of truth. So, while the balladeer has Michael, Lily and Skinner as 'heroes' and even, as he becomes increasingly sodden, republican 'volunteers', and while the judge brands them 'terrorists', and while the priest hails them as 'heroic' martyrs, we *know* (because we have unmediated access to them) that they fulfil none of these stereotypes; indeed, we know the preposterous exorbitancy of these claims. This is not to say that the characters are themselves guarantors of a transcendental meaning or truth; indeed, what becomes clear in the course of their few hours holed up in the Mayor's Parlour is a radical confusion about their own and their fellows' motivations for protesting. Nor are they immune to the clichéd language pertaining in post-Bloody Sunday Derry from which Friel is so keen to escape. Michael (who has been, he says, on every march since Duke Street, 5 October 1968) is the keenest to talk up the integrity of their struggle in terms that are unequivocally liberal/reformist:

> MICHAEL: . . . It was a good, disciplined, responsible march. And that's what we must show them – that we're responsible and respectable; and they'll come to respect what we're campaigning for . . . Do you go on all the marches, Lily?
> LILY: Most of them. It's the only exercise I get.
> MICHAEL: Do you have the feeling they're not as – I don't know – as dignified as they used to be? Like, d'you remember in the early days, they wouldn't even let you carry a placard – wouldn't even let you talk, for God's sake! And that was really impressive – all those people marching along in silence, rich and poor, high and low, doctors, accountants, plumbers, teachers, bricklayers – all shoulder to shoulder – knowing that what they wanted was their rights and knowing that because it was their rights nothing in the world was going to stop them from getting them.
> SKINNER: Shite – if you'll excuse me, Missus. Who's for more municipal booze?

Lily sets out her own reasons for marching in equally clichéd terms:

> SKINNER: Why did you march today?
> LILY: Sure everybody was marching the day.
> SKINNER: Why were you out?
> LILY: For the same reason as everybody else.
> SKINNER: Tell me your reasons.
> LILY: My reasons is no different to anybody else.
> SKINNER: Tell me yours.

LILY: Wan man – wan vote – that's what I want. You know – wan man – wan vote.
SKINNER: You got that six months ago.[13]
   (*Pause.*)
LILY: Sure I know that. Sure I know we got it.
SKINNER: That's not what you're marching for, then.
LILY: Gerrymandering – that's another thing – no more gerry-mandering – that's what I want – no more gerrymandering. And civil rights for everybody – that's what I want – you know – civil rights – civil rights – that's why I march.
SKINNER: I don't believe a word of it, Lily.

In supplying Lily with her 'real' reasons for protesting, Skinner actually comes closest to explaining his own motivations. His explanation that she marches as a protest against the impoverished conditions in which she, her eleven children and her invalid husband live is astute, but still he misses the point. Although she initially assents to his opinion, his suasive discourse actually overrides her. In fact, Lily's motives have very little to do – finally – with poverty, housing, gerrymandering, or the local government voting system: she marches for reasons that are entirely and uniquely her own. And in setting these out she finally escapes the stereo-typed discourse to which for almost all of her time in the Guildhall she so readily conforms:

LILY: I told you a lie about our Declan . . . He's not just shy, our Declan. He's a mongol . . . And it's for him I go on all the civil rights marches. Isn't that stupid? You and [Michael] and everybody else marching and protesting about sensible things like politics and stuff and me in the middle of you all, marching for Declan. Isn't that the stupidest thing you ever heard? Sure I could march and protest from here to Dublin and sure what good would it do Declan? Stupid and all as I am I know that much. But still I march – every Saturday. I still march.

And that, more or less, is it as far as the discussion of civil rights goes. There is no other reference to the political conflict that by 1970 would have been developing apace on the streets around them and, similarly, there is not, apart from the drunken balladeer's hagiography of Lily, Michael and Skinner, a word on the national question. His characterisa-tion of them as volunteers fighting for Mother Ireland is risible, but no more so than the judge's verdict based on his unquestioning acceptance of the brigadier's testimony that they came out of the Guildhall firing their non-existent guns. In fact each of the subsidiary characters acts out a rigidly predictable position: the British soldiers are foul-mouthed and aggressive; the RTÉ commentator is painfully deferential to church and state authority; the brigadier is a liar; the balladeer is a drunk; and the judge has come to his own conclusions about Lily, Michael and

Skinner's guilt even before the evidence has been presented to him. It is this patently satirical dimension of the play that seems to cause Friel so much of a problem: the anxiety he displays seems to be bound up in the question of whether or not, in attempting to transcend or escape 'clichéd articulation' (which is, according to Martin Amis the *raison d'être* of all literary artists), he has produced anything other than a play populated with Brechtian stereotypes? And certainly, at times, the play does feel like a piece of agitprop. However, things are more complex than that term would seem to imply.

Friel valorises eyewitness testimony over all other discourses. The voices and actions of the three main protagonists are chaotic, humane, funny and desperate. Everything they do and say is a form of testimony that is set against the official and authoritative versions of their behaviour and motivations. With the possible exception of the analysis of the sociologist, Dr Dodds, everything that is offered as evidence, that is taken as truth, is predictable and stereotyped. But it is precisely in revealing both the ease and the violence in this act of translation – how human frailty, desperation and, indeed, aspiration is transformed into stereotype – that the power of Friel's play is to be found. Lionel Pilkington argues similarly when he suggests that the play itself is a form of mimic-tribunal, in which the truth-producing strategies of powerful voices are revealed to the audience, who are placed in the position of quasi-jurists:

> Instead of concentrating the audience's attention on what might happen to the three civilians, therefore, Friel's play recasts the spectator in the role of the adjudicator. The spectator's role is presented as one of assessing and reviewing as evidence a wide range of speculative and 'objective' accounts made by those who remain outside the Guildhall. Encouraged to compare what can be seen and heard to take place in the Mayor's Parlour with the main verbal commentaries and assessments of this action that are made from the outside, this dramaturgical method comes to a head when what the audience can see and hear in the theatre is contradicted by the Judge's conclusions exonerating the army. In the final scene, the spectator witnesses Lily and the others with their hands above their heads – clearly unarmed – and then a fifteen second burst of gunfire. That the three civilians are innocent appears as obvious as the immediacy and the transparency of the spectator's perception.[14]

The nature of the major characters' testimony is complicated somewhat by the fact that they are dead. Every word produced by Lily, Michael and Skinner is spectral: this is an unavoidable consequence of the opening tableau, in which 'three bodies lie grotesquely across the front of the stage'. The fact that they are already dead as the play begins and that they continue, nevertheless, to address each other (and at one extraordinary moment, us) produces effects that can only be described as uncanny. As an audience we tend to get round this problem by thinking the play's structure in terms of flashbacks but the fact remains that, in inscribing their deaths at the beginning of the play, Friel enforces a structure that renders them powerless. Several critics have argued that the play's dramatic force is diminished by the fact that Lily, Skinner and Michael are already dead, but this is to fail to fully acknowledge the force of spectral uncanniness. The moment when the three characters, facing the audience (and speaking, as the stage directions tell us, 'calmly, without emotion, in neutral accents'), describe their deaths is an unforgettable moment of theatre:

> MICHAEL: We came out the front door as we had been ordered and stood on the top step with our hands above our heads. They beamed searchlights on our faces but I could see their outlines as they crouched beside their tanks. I even heard the click of their rifle-bolts. But there was no question of their shooting. Shooting belonged to a totally different order of things. And then the Guildhall Square exploded and I knew a terrible mistake had been made. And I became very agitated, not because I was dying, but that this terrible mistake be recognised and acknowledged. My mouth kept trying to form the word mistake – mistake – mistake. And that is how I died – in disbelief, in astonishment, in shock. It was a foolish way for a man to die.

> · · ·

> LILY: The moment we stepped outside the front door I knew I was going to die, instinctively, the way an animal knows. Jesus, they're going to murder me. A second of panic – no more. Because it was succeeded, overtaken, overwhelmed by a tidal wave of regret, not for myself nor my family, but that life had somehow eluded me. And now it was finished; it had all seeped away; and I had never experienced it. And in the silence before my body disintegrated in a purple convulsion, I thought I glimpsed a tiny truth: that life had eluded me because never once in my forty-three years had an experience, an event, even a small unimportant happening been isolated and assessed and articulated. And the fact that this, my last experience, was denied by this perception, this was the culmination of sorrow. In a way I died of grief.

> · · ·

> SKINNER: A short time after I realised we were in the Mayor's Parlour I knew that a price would be exacted. And when they ordered us a second time to lay down our arms I began to suspect what that price would be because they leave nothing to chance and because the poor are always overcharged. And as we stood on the Guildhall steps, two thoughts raced through my mind: how seriously they took us and how unpardonably casual we were about them; and that to match their seriousness would demand a total dedication, a solemnity as formal as theirs. And then everything melted and

fused in a great soaring heat. And my last thought was: if you're going to decide to take them on, Adrian Casimir, you've got to mend your ways. So I died, as I lived, in defensive flippancy.

Even in death there are multiple perspectives at work here. And there is a sense of developing insight after death, of truths arrived at after death as well as at the moment of death itself. In dying, Michael, in keeping with his thoroughly decent reformist politics, holds on to the 'cock-up' version of events, in which a 'mistake' has been made, but this becomes augmented by a later insight that this 'was a foolish way for a man to die'. Lily is overwhelmed by a sense of loss – but not to do with wealth or opportunity, but that not once in her life had anything, 'an experience, an event, even a small unimportant happening been isolated and assessed and articulated'. Skinner, too, experiences regret, but his regret has to do with not taking seriously the force at the disposal of the British. His elliptical sentiments can be read in a number of ways: the most obvious that he has come to realise, albeit belatedly, the necessity of deploying means as serious as the soldiers and the state they act for: 'to match their seriousness would demand a total dedication, a solemnity as formal as theirs'. These moving articulations of self-knowledge should not unnecessarily substantialise the characters as guarantors of meaning, nor should it mean that their rambling, funny, conversation in the Mayor's Parlour be reified as the truth of the play: very often, as we've already suggested, they reveal themselves as confused, not-knowing and just plain wrong.

Such a moment (where the dead describe their own deaths) is available only in art, and here, again, is a major reason for the distancing that occurs in, and is so important to the playwright in relation to, *The Freedom of the City*. It is barely conceivable that such a moment could be produced in relation to the actual Bloody Sunday dead, although of course Thomas Kinsella comes close when his ghosts are identifiable (as much as ghosts can be identified) as the spectres of particular individuals shot dead on the day. But the ethics of ventriloquism, of speaking through or on behalf of the silenced, smacks of a type of rejuvenation, a rhetorical rebirth into language and therefore agency in which the dead have the ability to comment on their own deaths, to speak back to power, to explain their actions and reactions, to attest their own innocence. The dead of Bloody Sunday possessed no such agency; there was no opportunity for them to voice their condition, to summarise their lives, to comment on the unfairness of the circumstances in which they found themselves, or to refute the grotesqueness of their characterisation in Widgery.

The force of spectrality in Friel's play deserves a little more attention. The speeches of the dead represent only the very beginnings of trauma. The three characters will have to act out (repeat and therefore relive) this moment time and again, and such a repetition is symptomatic of traumatised memory. Trauma, as Cathy Caruth argues, is the replaying and reliving of events that whilst happening are ungraspable, are ununderstandable, are, in their happening, beyond knowledge. Trauma for Caruth – following Freud – is the coming to knowledge of the event of violence, the coming to knowledge through repetition.[15] Such is the fate of Michael, Lily and Skinner. Fated to repeat the moment of annihilation they become the impossible witnesses of the wrong perpetrated against them. In the absence of any other attentive voice, it is only through their ghostly words that we, and they, come to realise the extent of the double injustice carried out against them: the first by the soldiers, the second by the apparatuses of the state. 'We speak in wounds', says one of the ghosts in Kinsella's *Butcher's Dozen*. In its terrible repetition, every time *The Freedom of the City* is performed or read (or thought) we experience trauma without healing – with no prospect or possibility of healing. The play itself is traumatised – the play itself *is* trauma.

Friel's attempt to distance his play from the specifics of Bloody Sunday by setting the play in 1970 produces startling historical and political effects. By imagining a Bloody Saturday occurring in Derry in early 1970 Friel accelerates history by condensing into the space of a few months what in fact took over two years to occur. If, by January 1972, relations between the British Army and the nationalist population of Derry were entirely antagonistic, the same could not be said for the situation in the city in February 1970. Although the so-called honeymoon period following their deployment on the streets of Belfast and Derry in August of the previous year had well and truly dissipated, as the army, under pressure from both the Westminster and Stormont governments, began to assert its authority by patrolling the no-go areas of Free Derry and by becoming involved with policing issues in the city centre, nothing approaching the seriousness of internment without trial had yet occurred. And whereas, by January 1972, the British Army had shot dead several civilians in the city (including Seamus Cusack, Desmond Beattie, Hugh Herron and Annette McGavigan), the most notable event to have occurred by February 1970 was the army's brutal response to nationalist demonstrations against an address by Ian Paisley. This incident, which began in Guildhall Square as a group of youths raised a tricolour during Paisley's speech, resulted in the first major incursion of the British Army into the Bogside, as the soldiers chased and attacked the retreating protestors. A number of commentators at the time noted that this incident marked a discernible hardening of attitudes of people living in Free Derry towards the army, who were beginning to be seen, not as neutral peacekeepers, but as a repressive force that was now carrying out the orders of the Stormont government much in the same way as the RUC and B-Specials had earlier carried out its bidding, with such disastrous results.

This is the precise moment in which *The Freedom of the City* is located. And by setting this fictional civil rights march and subsequent violent events in such a moment, Friel produces a scenario *ante factum* – a vision of British rule in Ireland that has remained virtually uncommented upon by critics of the play. The actions of the army and the judiciary in murdering and then traducing innocent victims, *The Freedom of the City* suggests, are predicated not on the deteriorating relationships with the nationalist/Catholic population, and not on the developing IRA campaign against the presence of the army in Northern Ireland (a campaign that by January 1972 was developing apace), but on a fundamental ideological division of subjects as either civilians or barbarians. The border between these positions is rigid and non-negotiable, in line with the original designation of 'barbarian' as one who was (a) not a Greek and then, more pointedly, as (b) one who lived outside the pale of the Roman empire and its civilisation. The citizens of Free Derry (those who lived outside the city, beyond the walls of the citadel) would not (indeed, could not, by the very nature of their barbarism) conform to the civic imperatives of the city and were therefore not citizens at all, but 'rude, wild, uncivilised persons'.[16] This, in itself, is enough to earn the contempt of the forces of the civic state, but Lily, Michael and Skinner do more than this. First they have the effrontery to protest and by so doing request that the conditions of civilisation are extended to those unfortunate enough to live outside the walls of the citadel, and then (albeit accidentally and chaotically) they find themselves within (even though the building is, paradoxically, without the city walls) the 'holiest of holies', Derry's Guildhall. Once they are there, as Skinner so accurately realises, their fate was settled and, yes, a price would have to be exacted for an act of such gross impertinence.

Enigmas of survival: *Carthaginians*

It seems almost by accident that Bloody Sunday intrudes upon the world of Frank McGuinness's seven protagonists in *Carthaginians*. Camped out in three plastic benders of the type used, the stage directions state, by the women of Greenham Common, Maela, Greta and Sarah, having seen a vision, now await an even more momentous event: the rising of the dead. Attending them in various roles (constructing a pyramid out of Derry's detritus, collecting flowers into plastic bags, hauling clay in a wheelbarrow), Paul, Seph and Hark share their patch of the City Cemetery in the Creggan. Providing all of them with food, drink, cigarettes, newspapers and gossip is Dido. Having much in common with Pyper in McGuinness's masterpiece, *Observe the Sons of Ulster Marching Towards the Somme* (1985), Dido is instrumental in providing a sceptical, humorous and unapologetically queer perspective on the actions of the men and women in the graveyard, who, much in the manner of Beckett's protagonists, seem to have suffered overwhelming personal traumas with little prospect of amelioration other than the hoped-for return of the dead.

McGuinness's drama unfolds over a week of glorious weather in late July or August of 1985: the summer of the moving statues. On the make, as ever, Dido is acting as publicist for the women, whose vigil is in danger of passing almost unnoticed:

> MAELA: Was anybody asking for us in town?
> DIDO: Nobody. You're kinda stake news now. But the rest of the world's beginning to take an interest . . .
> *Dido flamboyantly produces an* Irish Press.
> My media bombardment is starting to pay off. Page seven.
> *Dido gives Greta the paper.*
> GRETA: (reading) 'Graveyard Girls Greet the Ghosts. Three Derry Women have solved those holiday blues by turning into ghostbusters. They are sitting in Creggan graveyard in Derry waiting for the dead to rise. A spokesman for the girls, Mr Dido Martin, said, "They have seen a vision. Forget moving statues and Maggiagore [*sic*], this is the big one."'
> SARAH: You should be shot, young fella.
> DIDO: Read on Greta . . .
> GRETA: '"The girls may be suffering from illlusions," Mr Martin added. "They are simple but sincere souls, and each has endured a great personal tragedy," he concluded. We say, good luck, Ghost-busters, and if the dead rise, let us know.' Someone here is about to endure a great personal tragedy, and it's not one of the simple but sincere souls. What the hell are you up to?
> DIDO: Typical, typical. I'm doing my best. I need to rouse national interest. Nobody believes you in Derry, they thinks you're lunatics. The Catholics think you're mad, and the Prods thinks you're Martians.

Without the assistance and the presence of Dido the situation in which the other characters find themselves would be almost unbearable. Dido, gay, funny, rude, outrageous, resilient, mercantile and (importantly) much younger than the others, will play a key role in the fragile sense of resolution that does finally come about at the play's conclusion. Like Pyper, Dido queers most of the pieties and shibboleths that sustain what goes by the name of politics in the North. But this he does from an ethical position. Flying by the nets of conventional gender and sexual identity, Dido sees himself as a particular kind of freedom fighter: 'my ambition', he says, 'is to corrupt every member of Her Majesty's forces serving in Northern Ireland . . . It's my bit for the cause of Ireland's freedom. When the happy day of withdrawal comes, I'll be venerated as a national hero.'

Each of McGuinness's characters carries their own burden: Seph lives with the guilt of being an informer; Hark lives with his inability to take up the gun; Paul, who was once a teacher, is victim to a severe post-traumatic stress disorder brought about by the Troubles; Greta has suffered a major breakdown in circumstances that are not altogether clear; and Sarah has battled with drug addiction. Most harrowingly, Maela has lost her daughter and it is around the child's grave that the action of the play revolves. Maela dresses the grave and talks to it, as she would her daughter, and it is the promise of the child's return in particular that seems to galvanise the women into action.

To pass the time before the expected vision occurs, the characters tell dirty jokes, collect leaves, build the pyramid, rehearse questions and answers from Derry pub quizzes, smoke cigarettes, attend to a dying blackbird and, at Dido's insistence, take part in an excruciating burlesque of the Troubles. Set in Derry, *The Burning Balaclava* by Fionnuala McGonigle, which is, it turns out, a *nom de plume* for Dido himself (whose 'real' name we never get to know; the appelation 'Dido' has been conferred upon him by a Lebanese sailor), does everything to subvert the pieties of almost every party to the North's political conflict. Dido's play is in, as Susan Cannon Harris argues, a complex and somewhat troubled relationship to the wider performances of political and gender identity that it distils.[17] Inviting his friends to follow his own 'real-life' performances of drag, Dido/McGonigle creates a pastiche of stock characters acting out political, gender and sectarian stereotypes. The violently homophobic Hark plays the heroine, Mrs Doherty, 'a fifty-year-old Derry mother, tormented by the troubles'; Maela, who displays no political interest whatsoever, plays Mrs Doherty's idealistic and patriotic son Padraig O'Dochartaigh, who, shawled in a gigantic tricolour, is 'tormented by the troubles of his native land' and by moral dilemmas such as '[s]hould he or should he not take up the gun for Ireland? Should he or should he not speak Gaelic all the time. Should he or should he not screw his girlfriend, a Protestant, Mercy Dogherty', who is played by Paul. Mercy's father, an RUC man, who, 'when he interrogates Catholic suspects . . . beats them over the head with the crucifix and strangles them with the rosary beads to make them confess', is played by Greta. Seph, who is silent for almost the entire duration of *Carthaginians*, plays Father O'Docherty, 'tormented because [his] weekly calls from the pulpit for peace and reconciliation have for so long gone unheard' so that now he has 'stopped speaking entirely and . . . communicate[s] only by means of white flags'. Sarah plays Jimmy Doherty, who, 'tormented by the fact that all his life he has been out of work', spends his 'time walking the dog and washing the wains and drinking in pubs telling yarns and singing songs'. 'He's a Derry character', Dido informs Sarah, 'but don't worry, he's the first to be killed'. Dido plays two parts himself: Doreen O'Doherty, 'driven to distraction by the troubles', and a 'British soldier, nameless, faceless, in enemy uniform, in deep torment because he is a working-class cockney sent here to oppress the working class'. Dido's drama results in the predictable bloodbath: the English soldier shoots Doreen's dog, Charlie. Doreen joins the IRA 'for Charlie'. The RUC man shoots Jimmy for singing Phil Coulter's 'The Town I Loved So Well'. The priest is shot dead as he attempts to broker an agreement between, on one side of the street, Mrs Doherty and Padraig, and, on the other, Mercy and her RUC father. And then, in a moment reminiscent of the catastrophe of *Hamlet*, the real bloodletting begins:

> MAELA: We've shot a priest, we've shot a priest.
> PAUL: He's not a priest, he's not a priest.
> MAELA: How is he not a priest.
> PAUL: He's not waving a white flag.
> (MAELA *shoots* PAUL.)
> MAELA: Blasphemer, you've shot a priest.
> (GRETA *shoots* MAELA.)
> GRETA: Catholic bastard, you've shot my daughter.
> (HARK *shoots* GRETA.)
> HARK: You murdering RUC madman. Look at this. All dead. Dead. What could I do? I had to kill. I depend on the dying. Nobody knew it, not even my son, but I knit all the balaclavas. The more that dies, the more I'm given. Violence is terrible, but it pays well.
> (DIDO *shoots* HARK.)
> DIDO: What could I do? I'm only a soldier. A working-class boy, just a boy.
> What does Ireland mean to me? What does it all mean?
> (*They all rise and shoot* DIDO.)
> The've got me. I join the dying. What's a Brit under the clay? What's a Protestant in the ground? What's a Catholic in the grave? All the same. Dead. All dead. We're all dead. They've got me. It's over. It's over. (*Dies.*)
> That's it. What did you think?
> (*Silence.*)
> Tell me the truth. Isn't it just like real life?
> (*Silence.*)

The death of the white-flag-waving priest – echoing, as it does, one of the most iconic images of Bloody Sunday – alerts us to the startling possibility that here, in a farce acted out in the graveyard where most of the victims lay buried, something quite different from the usual reverence that marks each and every representation of the Paras' attack on the protestors may be occurring. Susan Cannon Harris argues that this risky strategy has as its target, not just contemporary interpretations of Bloody Sunday itself, but a history of theatrical representation:

> Dido's parody is, among other things, an indictment of Irish drama as one of the perpetrators of the various kinds of trouble plaguing Derry. *The Burning Balaclava* conflates skewed allusions to both contemporary treatments of Bloody Sunday and the Troubles and to

Irish Renaissance-era dramas, ranging from what may be a covert
reference to Brian Friel's *The Freedom of the City* (which also features a middle-aged Derry wife and mother named Doherty) to a
number of allusions to O'Casey's *Juno and the Paycock*. As Culling-
ford argues, *The Burning Balaclava* suggests that O'Casey's mistake
was sharing and reinscribing nationalist dependence on exactly what
Dido is working against the 'sentimental overestimation of Irish
motherhood and . . . the essentialist myth of Mother Ireland'.
Carthaginians is an attempt to correct that mistake, but like *The
Burning Balaclava* and *Juno and the Paycock* it cannot avoid participating, however ironically, in the tradition it seeks to subvert, and
risking a repetition of the plot it wants to undo.[18]

We would, however, question Harris's conflation of *The Burning
Balaclava* and *Carthaginians*, and not simply in their supposedly shared
participation, even in ironic terms, in a tradition that promotes a
'sentimental overestimation of Irish motherhood and . . . the essentialist
myth of Mother Ireland'. The sheer grotesqueness of Dido's farce – not
least its *coup de théâtre*, in which it is revealed that Mrs O'Doherty is
among the chief sponsors of and profiteers from the conflict – would
not particularly seem to run the risk of repeating the old story of Mother
Ireland/Cathleen Ni Houlihan. And Harris's argument becomes even
harder to sustain when we turn to *Carthaginians* itself, especially in
relation to its complex melding of personal and communal narratives
centred on the events in Derry on 30 January 1972.

It is the almost-silent Seph – silent because he spoke to the wrong
people, silent because he informed – who breaks the silence on Bloody
Sunday:

> SARAH: Why did you come back here to live?
> SEPH: I lived here, I was born here. I was here one Sunday. Sunday.
> I saw it. Bloody Sunday. I was in Derry on Bloody Sunday.
> GRETA: Bloody Sunday. Where were you on Bloody Sunday?
> PAUL: Here. I was here.
> HARK: On the march.
> SARAH: Through Derry.
> GRETA: Were we all there?
>   (*Silence.*)
> Were we all here on Bloody Sunday?
> SEPH: Everything changed after Bloody Sunday.
> MAELA: Nothing changed. Nothing happened that day. Nobody
> died. I should know. I was in the hospital. If there had been anyone
> dead I would have seen them. And I saw no one dead. You're telling
> lies. You've driven away the dead. I hope you're satisfied. I hope
> you're satisfied with your lies.

Addressed as it is to deeply traumatised and compromised people, Greta's
repeated question takes on a palpably coercive force; yet it is not met by

an answer but by Seph's truism. What will become clear throughout the remainder of *Carthaginians* is the multiplicity of responses to 30 January 1972 that puts into question any automatic assumption that Bloody Sunday impacted uniformly on those who were – or were not – there.

Maela's apparently irrational rebuttal of Seph's statement articulates, as the audience will find out soon enough, the terrible circumstances of her daughter's death:

> MAELA: My wee girl's dead. They're running mad through the streets of Derry and my daughter's dead. Do you not understand that? . . . I went for a walk. Through Derry. Everyone was crying. What was wrong with them? All shouting . . . They said, 'She's dead. I'm afraid she's dead. We can get you home safely in an ambulance. There's a lot of bother stirring in the town.' I said, 'What do you mean she's dead?' . . . Everybody's running and everybody's crying. What's wrong? Why cry? Two dead, I hear that in William Street. I'm walking through Derry and they're saying in Shipquay Street there's five dead . . . I am in Ferryquay Street and I hear there's nine dead outside the Rosville [*sic*] flats. They opened fire and shot them dead. No, nobody's dead. My daughter's not dead. Where are there dead in Derry? Let me look on the dead. Jesus, the dead. The innocent dead. There's thirteen dead in Derry . . . She had fire. She opened fire on herself. When I wasn't looking she caught cancer. It burned her. She was thirteen. It was Sunday.

Nowhere in the play is there a more devastating articulation of the force of Cathy Caruth's observation that 'trauma is not locatable in the simple violent or original event in an individual's past, but rather in the way that its very unassimilated nature – the way it was precisely *not known* in the first instance – returns to haunt the survivor later on'.[19] Clearly, we do not have access to the world Maela inhabited before she began her vigil in the City Cemetery, but the confusion and non-concatenation of her language in this extract suggest that her trauma has not even begun to be addressed.

Maela is not the only person whose experience of Bloody Sunday cannot be easily narrativised into a coherent account of the day's meanings. Seph raises questions that suggest an almost blasphemous understanding of Bloody Sunday:

> SEPH: Would it have been better to have been shot on Bloody Sunday? Did I want that to happen? Why did we all want it? Did we want Bloody Sunday to happen?
> HARK: How the hell could we want Bloody Sunday to happen?
> SEPH: So we could make sense of it all, make sense of our suffering. (*Starts to wrap the tricolour round the guitar.*) Thirteen dead on Bloody Sunday. It could have been thirteen hundred. Thirteen thousand. Thirteen million. One. One left alive, that one is me and I'm going to tell.

HARK: You've told enough.
SEPH: Have I told you this? Listen. *(Batters the ground with the guitar wrapped in the tricolour.)* That's the war in my head. They said after Bloody Sunday they wanted to avenge the dead but they wanted to join them. And I would tell on the living who wanted to join the dead. I'd save them from themselves. I'd save them from the dead . . .
HARK: You were a traitor. Nothing else.

McGuinness's play seems to be a voicing of unrelieved trauma. There are diversions and there is laughter but, as in Beckett, such actions serve to furnish merely a temporary forgetting. Only Dido, who was a child at the time of Bloody Sunday, ecapes the debilitating effects the day has had. But we want to suggest that through the 'work' involved in acting out his *The Burning Balaclava* the characters, who until then have borne individually their several burdens, merge into a collectivity, with startling results. In the final moments of the play they again perform in chorus, producing effects that are both uncanny and deeply moving. Towards its ending *Carthaginians* seems to shift from dramatic theatre to poetry. At first the shift seems casual enough, but, within seconds of Paul and Seph discussing their admiration of poetry, the names of the Bloody Sunday dead are recited by Paul. In the first published version of the play the names are punctuated by characters questioning the effects of Bloody Sunday upon their own lives, but in McGuinness's preferred version, the names of the dead retain an integrity by being recited in exactly the same fashion as every commemorative vigil at the memorial at Joseph Place:

PAUL: Do remember their names? The dead of Bloody Sunday?
   (Silence).
PAUL: Bernard McGuigan, forty-one years, Inishcairn Gardens, Derry. Patrick Doherty, thirty years [sic], Hamilton Street, Derry. Michael Kelly, seventeen, from Dunmore Gardens, Derry. William McKinney, twenty-seven, from Westway, Derry. James Wray, twenty-three [sic], Drumcliffe Avenue, Derry. Hugh Gilmore [sic], seventeen years old, Garvan Place, Derry. Jack Duddy, who was seventeen, Central Drive, Derry. William Nash, nineteen, Dunree Gardens, Derry. Michael McDaid, twenty-one [sic], Tyrconnell Street, Derry. Gerald Donaghy, seventeen, Meenan Square, Derry. John Young, seventeen, Westway, Derry. Kevin McElhinney [sic], seventeen, Philip Street, Derry. Gerald McKinney, Knockdara House, Waterside, Derry.
HARK: Perpetual light shine upon you. Rest in peace.
SEPH: Bloody Sunday.
SARAH: Sunday.
GRETA: Sunday.
SARAH: Sunday.
GRETA: Wash the dead.
PAUL: Bury the dead.

SEPH: Sunday.
SARAH: Raise the dead.
HARK: Sunday.
DIDO: Do you see the dead?
GRETA: The dead beside you.
MAELA: The dead behind you.
SARAH: The dead before you.
GRETA: Forgive the dead.
MAELA: Forgive the dying.
SARAH: Forgive the living.
PAUL: Forgive yourself.
HARK: Forgive yourself.
SEPH: Forgive yourself.
MAELA: Bury the dead.
GRETA: Raise the living.
SARAH: Wash the living.

> *Light breaks through the graveyard.*
> *Birdsong begins.*
> *Light illuminates them all.*
> *They listen, looking at each other, in the light.*
> *They lie down and sleep.*

The delicacy of McGuinness's writing allows an inference that what the women have been waiting for has indeed come to pass, while at the same time suggesting that a resolution of sorts has occurred, without the necessity for spectral apparitions or revenance of the dead. The final words certainly suggest an adaptation to material circumstances – that the dead do indeed remain dead, and that it is the living to whom we should most carefully attend – but the visual effects leave the question wide open. Describing *Carthaginians* as 'my elegy to the dead and the living of Derry, the living who kept going, in Dido's words, "Surviving. Carthage has not been destroyed"',[20] the playwright is clearly at pains to stress the resilience of both the survivors of Bloody Sunday and members of that community so grievously injured on that day. Dido's final words are, indeed, a valediction to Derry (or a certain part of Derry). But in leaving, his apostrophe to the city insists on its continuity and humour, rather than defeat or depression: traits to which the play of which he is the most extraordinary element seems, at times, in danger of succumbing:

DIDO: Well, I believe it is time to leave Derry. Love it or leave it. Now or never . . . Why am I talking to myself in a graveyard? Because everyone in Derry talks to themselves. Everybody in the world talks to themselves. What's the world? Shipquay Street and Ferryquay Street and Rosville [*sic*] Street and William Street and the Strand and Great James Street. While I walk the earth, I walk through you, the streets of Derry. If I meet one who knows you and they ask, 'How's Dido?' Surviving. How's Derry? Surviving. Surviving. Carthage has not been destroyed.

Staging the inquiry – *Bloody Sunday: Scenes from the Saville Inquiry*

Lord Saville's letter of 24 October 2006 to the families, in which he explains the reasons for the further delay in the publication of his report, sets out the daunting mass of evidence which the Bloody Sunday inquiry has to process before it delivers the 'definitive' version of both the events and the contributory factors leading to the shooting dead of thirteen people and the injuring of a similar number in Derry on 30 January 1972. In our Introduction we quoted from this letter and we want to return to it briefly to stress the process through which – as we conclude this book – the inquiry team continues to work. The delays, Saville assures the families, are due not just to the sheer amount of material, but to the interpretative tasks presented by it:

> The tribunal has the formidable task of analysing this vast amount of evidence, assessing the reliability of the witnesses, determining so far as possible where the truth lies on hundreds of disputed issues, and giving a full and clear explanation of its reasoning and conclusions.[21]

The transcripts on the official Bloody Sunday inquiry website[22] constitute a veritable heteroglossia, in which the multiple truths of Bloody Sunday are laid bare before the inquiry's processes of selection, interpretation, and narrativisation shape them into a 'version'. This is not to say that *every* truth is to be found amongst the evidence and submissions: certain key pieces of evidence (such as the rifles used on the day and subsequently held in the safe-keeping of the British Ministry of Defence) disappeared in decidely suspicious circumstances before they could be presented and properly analysed by the inquiry. Photographic evidence available from the ten military photographers on duty in Derry on Bloody Sunday has also been destroyed.[23]

Richard Norton-Taylor's drama, *Bloody Sunday: Scenes from the Saville Inquiry* (2005), is made up of twelve heavily edited exchanges between witnesses to the events of 30 January 1972 and the lawyers representing the families and soldiers. Reconstructing the inquiry with the utmost sense of verisimilitude – the stage is packed with lawyers' desks, boxes of files, computer screens and audio-visual technologies (even the squeaking door of the Great Hall of the Guildhall is included amongst the performance's sound-effects, as is the 'soothing' music of Vivaldi that played before the hearings began each morning) – some of the most familiar moments from the four years of hearings are included. There is Bishop Edward Daly suggesting to Edwin Glasgow, QC, that the men of violence 'were not just civilians . . . And men of violence on that particular day certainly were those in uniforms'.[24] There is Michael Bridge's memorable response to Christopher Clarke's question concerning the targets at whom the soldiers were firing:

> BRIDGE: I seen them firing, I seen them firing. What they were firing at is, effectively I cannot tell you, but in a situation like that, you would assume that they were firing at you, that would be the impression.[25]

Bernadette McAliskey's vituperative performance is captured, as are the quieter testimonies of William McDonagh, Alice Doherty and Geraldine McBride, all present on the day of the march. Norton-Taylor's severe editing works best, we would argue, where the senior and junior members of the British Army are cross-examined. For among the carefully rehearsed evasions and willed forgetfulness of the soldiers, moments of breakthrough are revealed: notably the fact, admitted by Major General Andrew MacLellan, that his orders on the necessity to effect an arrest operation rather than 'conduct a running battle down Rossville Street' had been broken. Similarly, Sir Robert Ford's role as an observer, who observed, by his own admission, 'nothing', and Colonel Derek Wilford's admission that he saw only '1%' of the activities of his own soldiers are depicted as a form of tragi-comedy.

The performance met with almost universal acclaim by critics, who agreed more or less completely with Michael Billington, who regarded it as 'political theatre at its very best'.[26] Billington continued:

> Theatre is a mansion with many rooms, and there is obviously a place for fictional political drama. But the great merit of this kind of tribunal drama is that it takes us behind closed doors and exposes the way in which a cataclysmic event like Bloody Sunday occurred. It also shows that in theatre nothing is as hypnotic as fact. You emerge from the event, after 2 hours, not only better informed, but feeling that, at its best, theatre is a vital part of a democratic society.

While there is much to commend such a view, Norton-Taylor's production raises several important issues and problems. In selecting only twelve out of over nine hundred cross-examinations, there is the inference that what we are seeing and hearing on stage has, somehow, a greater validity, or truth value, than those exchanges that did not make it into the drama, and that were not, perhaps, of sufficient dramatic resonance to make it into the drama. Clearly, the performance cannot replicate the entire proceedings of a tribunal of the scale and complexity of the Bloody Sunday inquiry, and clearly there is a case for condensing and editing those proceedings for dramatic effect. The price paid for that is, however, a gross simplification of the dialogism at work in the inquiry. The Bloody Sunday inquiry was far from 'an ideal speech situation' (indeed, Norton-Taylor, via the transcripts available on the inquiry's website, shows the very difficulty language has in articulating 'truth'), but it has been the most capacious and attentive form hitherto available. In this drama, written and presented for a British audience who would have very little acquaintance with the inquiry itself, the necessary simplification of an edited version may well be justifiable as a sort of *aide-mémoire*. But, for those with a deeper, long-standing and complex knowledge of, and investment in, the inquiry as an absolutely key component in the complex and delicate processes of truth-recovery/truth-creation, Norton-Taylor's production is little more than a journalistic intervention in the middle of this strange limbo-like period before Mark Saville produces his long-awaited report.

Notes and References

INTRODUCTION

1 John Passmore Widgery, *Bloody Sunday, 1972* (London: HMSO, 2001), p. 99. This was originally published as the *Report of the Tribunal appointed to inquire into the events on Sunday, 30 January 1972, which led to the loss of life in connection with the procession in Londonderry on that day by The Rt. Hon. Lord Widgery, OBE, TD* (London: HMSO, 1972).
2 Ibid., p. 100.
3 The long-standing logomachy over the name of the city of Derry/Londonderry/L'Derry is well known. Throughout this book we will be using the term 'Derry' to designate the mainly nationalist/Catholic section of that city; in other words, the part of the city that lies to the west of the River Foyle.
4 Just a week before Bloody Sunday, on Saturday 22 January 1972, 'an anti-internment march was held at Magilligan strand, County Derry, with several thousand people taking part. As the march neared the internment camp it was stopped by members of the Green Jackets and the Parachute Regiment of the British Army, who used barbed wire to close off the beach. When it appeared that the marchers were going to go around the wire, the army then fired rubber bullets and CS gas at close range into the crowd. A number of witnesses claimed that the paratroopers (who had been bused from Belfast to police the march) severely beat a number of protesters and had to be physically restrained by their own officers. John Hume accused the soldiers of "beating, brutalising and terrorising" the demonstrators' (http://cain.ulst.ac.uk/events/bsunday/chron.htm).
5 Edward Daly, *Mister, Are You a Priest?* (Dublin: Four Courts Press, 2000), p. 211.
6 Bloody Sunday Initiative, 'Programme of Events: Bloody Sunday 1972–1992' (1992), p. 1.
7 Tony Blair, *Parliamentary Debates (Hansard)*, Sixth Series, Vol. 305, Col. 502 (29 January 1998).
8 Mark Saville, 'Letter to Mr Michael McKinney and Mr John Kelly' (24 October 2006), p. 1.
9 Samuel Dash, *Justice Denied: A Challenge to Lord Widgery's report on 'Bloody Sunday'* (London: ILRM and NCCL, 1972), p. 11.
10 Don Mullan, *Eyewitness Bloody Sunday: The Truth* (London: Merlin, 2002), 3rd edition, p. 186.
11 Dermot Walsh, *Bloody Sunday and the Rule of Law in Northern Ireland* (Houndmills: Macmillan, 2000), pp. 76–80.
12 The phrase is Seamus Heaney's. See his Nobel lecture, 'Crediting Poetry', in *Opened Ground: Poems 1966–1996* (London: Faber, 1998), p. 456.
13 Eamonn McCann, (ed.), *The Bloody Sunday Inquiry: The Families Speak Out* (London: Pluto Press, 2006), p. 5.

14 Anne Crilly and Angela Hegarty, 'Remembering Bloody Sunday: The Role of Popular Culture in Legal Process'. Paper presented to the 2004 Socio-Legal Studies Association Conference, Glasgow, 6–8 April 2004.
15 Niall Ó Dochartaigh, *From Civil Rights to Armalites: Derry and the Birth of the Irish Troubles* (Cork: Cork University Press, 1997), p. 230.
16 McCann, *Bloody Sunday Inquiry* p. 5.

CHAPTER 1: TURBULENT TIMES

1 Trisha Ziff (ed.), *Hidden Truths: Bloody Sunday 1972* (Santa Monica: Smart Art Press, 1998), p. 35.
2 Manuel Delanda, *A Thousand Years of Nonlinear History* (New York: Swerve, 1997), p. 17.
3 Gilles Deleuze and Félix Guattari, *Kafka: Toward a Minor Literature* (Minneapolis: University of Minneapolis Press, 1986).
4 Manuel Delanda, 'Nonorganic Life', in J. Crary and S. Kwinter (eds), *Zone 6: Incorporations* (New York: Urzone, 1992), pp. 154–5.
5 Ó Dochartaigh, p. 61.
6 A term coined by Deleuze and Guattari. See their *A Thousand Plateaus* (London: The Athlone Press, 1988).
7 Bob Purdie, *Politics in the Streets: The Origins of the Civil Rights Movement in Northern Ireland* (Belfast: Blackstaff Press, 1990), p. 2.
8 Michael Hardt and Antonio Negri, *Empire* (Cambridge, MA: Harvard University Press, 2000), p. 261.
9 Niall Ó Dochartaigh, N. *From Civil Rights to Armalites: Derry and the Birth of the Irish Troubles* (Cork: Cork University Press, 1997), pp. 53-9
10 Michael McGuinness and Garghán Downey, *Creggan: More Than a History* (L'Derry: Guildhall Press, 2000), p. 239.
11 Purdie, p. 78.
12 Peter Goodrich, *Languages of Law: From Logics of Memory to Nomadic Masks* (London: Weidenfeld & Nicolson, 1990), p. 298.
13 Neil Jarman, *Material Conflicts: Parades and Visual Displays in Northern Ireland* (Oxford: Berg, 1997), p. 76.
14 Ibid., p. 78.
15 Jack Santino, *Signs of War and Peace: Social Conflict and the Uses of Symbols in Public in Northern Ireland* (New York: Palgrave Macmillan, 2001), p. 119.
16 Jarman, p. 152.
17 Paul Virilio, *Speed and Politics* (New York: Semiotext(e), 1986), p. 19.
18 Jarman, p. 79.
19 Gilles Deleuze and Félix Guattari, *A Thousand Plateaus*, p. 381.
20 Paddy Docherty, *Paddy Bogside* (Cork: Mercier Press, 2001), p. 151.
21 Hakim Bey, *T. A. Z. The Temporary Autonomous Zone, Ontological Anarchy, Poetic Terrorism* (Autonomedia Anti-copyright, 1985), (http://www.hermetic.com/bey/taz_cont.html).
22 Adrian Kerr (ed.), 'Introduction', *No Go: A Photographic Record of Free Derry* (L'Derry: Guildhall Press, 1997), pp. 4–5.
23 Paul Patton, *Deleuze and the Political* (London: Routledge, 2000), p. 11.
24 Deleuze and Guattari, *A Thousand Plateaus*, pp. 360–1.
25 Nick Thoburn, *Deleuze, Marx and Politics* (London: Routledge, 2003), p. 19.
26 Deleuze and Guattari, *A Thousand Plateaus*, p. 386.
27 Manuel Delanda, *War in the Age of Intelligent Machines* (New York: Zone Books, 1991), p. 8.
28 William G. Cunningham, 'Violent Conflict in Northern Ireland: Complex Life at the Edge of Chaos'. Paper presented to the 2001 National Conference on Peacemaking and Conflict Resolution (NCPCR), George Mason University, Fairfax, Virginia, 7–10 June 2001 (http://cain.ulst.ac.uk/conflict/index.html).

29 John Urry, 'The Complexity Turn', *Theory, Culture and Society* 22 (5): 2005, p. 1.
30 David Byrne, 'Complexity, Configurations and Cases', *Theory, Culture and Society* 22 (5): 2005, p. 97.
31 Cunningham, 'Violent Conflict'.
32 Pam Morris, *The Bakhtin Reader* (London and New York: Arnold, 1994), p. 225.
33 Peter Stallybrass and Allon White, *The Politics and Poetics of Transgression* (Ithaca: Cornell University Press, 1986), p. 14.
34 Ó Dochartaigh, p. 245.
35 Brian Massumi, *A User's Guide to Capitalism and Schizophrenia: Deviations from Deleuze and Guattari* (Cambridge, MA, and London: The MIT Press, 1992), p. 60.
36 David Byrne, *Complexity Theory and the Social Sciences: An Introduction* (Routledge, London, 1998), p. 4.
37 Cunningham, 'Violent Conflict'.
38 Delanda, 'Nonorganic Life' p. 138.
39 Byrne, *Complexity Theory*, p. 170.
40 Michael Serres, *Genesis* (Ann Arbor: University of Michigan Press, 1995), p. 59.
41 Virilio, *Speed and Politics*, p. 55.
42 Ibid., p. 120.
43 Cunningham, 'Violent Conflict'.
44 H. W. Jung, 'Bakhtin's Dialogical Body Politics', in M. M. Bell and M. Gardiner (eds.), *Bakhtin and the Human Sciences* (London: Sage, 1998), p. 107.

CHAPTER 2: FACES OF THE DEAD

 1 Walter Benjamin, 'Theses on the Philosophy of History', in H. Zorn (ed.), *Illuminations* (London: Pimlico, 1999), p. 226.
 2 Emmanuel Levinas, quoted in Tamra Wright, Peter Hughes, and Alison Ainley, 'The Paradox of Morality: An Interview with Emmanuel Levinas', in Robert Bernasconi and David Wood (eds.), *The Provocation of Levinas: Rethinking the Other* (London: Routledge, 1988), p. 169.
 3 Quoted in Zygmunt Bauman, *Postmodern Ethics* (Oxford: Blackwell, 1993), p. 73.
 4 John Tagg, *The Burden of Representation: Essays on Photographies and Histories* (Basingstoke: Macmillan, 1988), p. 56.
 5 Philippe Dubois, *L'Acte Photographique* (Paris and Brussels: Nathan/Labor, 1983).
 6 Roland Barthes, *Camera Lucida* (London: Vintage, 1993), p. 92.
 7 Susan Sontag, *On Photography* (London: Penguin, 1977), p. 154.
 8 Benjamin, p. 252.
 9 Jacques Derrida, *Specters of Marx: The State of the Debt, the Work of Mourning, and the New International* (New York and London: Routledge, 1994), p. 97.
10 Walsh, pp. 76–80.
11 Barthes, p. 47.
12 Bauman, p. 155.
13 *An Phoblacht/Republican News*, 23 May 2002 (http://republican-news.org/ archive/2002/ May23/23 ball.html).
14 George Rudé, *The Face of the Crowd: Studies in Revolution, Ideology and Popular Protest* (New York and London: Harvester Wheatsheaf, 1988), p. 6.
15 Ibid.
16 On the different emphases and conflicts between the various groups who contributed towards commemorative events, see Seamus Dunn, 'Bloody Sunday and Its Commemoration Parades', in T.G. Fraser, (ed.), *Irish Parading Tradition: Following the Drum* (Gordonsville, VA: Palgrave Macmillan, 2000), pp. 133–7.
17 Graham Dawson, 'Trauma, Place and the Politics of Memory: Bloody Sunday, Derry, 1972–2004', *History Workshop Journal* 59: 2005, pp. 165–6.
18 Graham Dawson, 'Father Daly's White Hanky: Survivor Memories, Collective Memory and the Postmemory of Bloody Sunday'. Paper given at the 'Hanky Day:

Recent Visual Representations of Conflict in Northern Ireland' symposium, Manchester Metropolitan University, 26 November 2005.

19 Elias Canetti, *Crowds and Power* (London: Phoenix Press, 2000), p. 63.

20 The *féile* is an annual week-long festival of arts, cultural and community activity organised by the Gasyard Development Trust in Derry.

21 Will Kelly. Email correspondence with the authors (30 November 2005).

22 Jarman, pp. 106–7.

23 Paul Ricoeur, 'Memory and Forgetting', in R. Kearney and M. Dooley (eds), *Questioning Ethics: Contemporary Debates in Continental Philosophy* (London: Routledge, 1998), p. 10.

CHAPTER 3: VIRTUAL JUSTICE

1 Jean-François Lyotard, *The Différend: Phrases in Dispute* (Minneapolis: University of Minnesota Press, 1988), p. 8.

2 Widgery, p. 97.

3 Dunn, p. 133.

4 Walsh, p. 85.

5 See the website (www.bloody-sunday-inquiry.org).

6 Bernadette Devlin, Testimony to the Saville inquiry, day 112, Tuesday 15 May 2001 (www.bloody-sunday-inquiry.org, TS112, 2001), p. 70.

7 Angela Hegarty, 'Truth, Law and Official Denial: The Case of Bloody Sunday', *Criminal Law Forum* 15 (1/2): 2004, p. 199.

8 Benjamin, p. 256.

9 Mariana Valverde, 'Derrida's Justice and Foucault's Freedom: Ethics, History, and Social Movements', *Law and Social Inquiry* 24 (3): 1999, p. 662.

10 Jacques Derrida, *Of Grammatology* (Baltimore and London: John Hopkins University Press, 1976), pp. 144–64.

11 Patrick Hayes and Jim Campbell, *Bloody Sunday: Trauma, Pain and Politics* (London: Pluto Press, 2005), p. 171.

12 Ibid., p. 91.

13 Ibid., p. 74.

14 Mullan, p. xlvii.

15 Cathy Caruth, *Unclaimed Experience: Trauma, Narrative, and History* (Baltimore and London: John Hopkins University Press, 1996), pp. 91–2.

16 Deleuze and Guattari, *A Thousand Plateaus*, pp. 15–16.

17 Ibid., p. 16.

18 Andrew Quick writes of this process: 'The authoritarian regime . . . relies on the mastery of time to differentiate itself from those that would challenge its authenticity and legitimacy. Time is converted into readable space. In this way the past can and must be accounted for. Events that trouble and destabilise a regime become negotiable through representational systems, through historical account, through judicial process, through legal and political enquiry. As a result of such systems everything becomes retrievable via the operation of a certain version of remembering that works to transform past events into a discernible present' ('The Space Between: Photography and the Time of Forgetting in the Work of Willie Doherty', in A. Kuhn and K.E. McAllister [eds], *Locating Memory: Photographic Acts* [New York and Oxford: Berghahn Books, 2006], p. 167).

19 Elizabeth Loftus, 'Our changeable memories: Legal and practical implications', *Nature Reviews Neuroscience* 4: March 2003, p. 23.

20 Richard Terdiman, *Present Past: Modernity and the Memory Crisis* (Ithaca and London: Cornell University Press, 1993), p. 8.

21 Hayes and Campbell, p. 166.

22 David Tereshchuk, 'Through a Glass Darkly: Memories of Bloody Sunday' (2006) (http://www.tereshchuk.com/go/on/archived/art/3845).

23 This term refers to the process by which contemporary events are presented through the tele-visual media as 'spectacles' stripped of any sense of historical location or

explanation. See Debord, G. *Society of the Spectacle* (New York: Zone Books, 1994).

24 Pierre Nora, 'Between Memory and History: *Les Lieux de Mémoire*', *Representations* 26: Spring 1989, p. 17.

25 Alan Megill, 'History, Memory, Identity', *History of the Human Sciences* 11 (3): 1998, p. 55.

26 Philip Auslander, *Liveness: Performance in a Mediatized Culture* (London and New York: Routledge, 1999), p. 127.

27 G. D.White, '"Quite a Profound Day": The Public Performance of Memory by Military Witnesses at the Bloody Sunday Tribunal', *Theatre Research International* 31 (2): 2006, p. 184.

28 Ricoeur, p. 5.

29 Ibid., p. 8.

30 Joanne O'Brien, *A Matter of Minutes: The Enduring Legacy of Bloody Sunday* (Dublin: Wolfhound Press, 2002), p. 91.

31 Megill, p. 56.

32 Liliane Weissberg and Dan Ben-Amos (eds.), 'Introduction', *Cultural Memory and the Construction of Identity* (Detroit: Wayne State University, 1999), p. 17.

33 Hayes and Campbell, p. xv.

34 This has been described as a contested realm between 'memory entrepreneurs'; L. Spillman and B. Conway, 'Texts, Bodies, and the Memory of Bloody Sunday', *Symbolic Interaction* 30 (1) 2007, p. 92.

35 Graham Dawson, 'Trauma, Memory, Politics: The Irish Troubles', in K. Rogers, (ed.), *Trauma and Life Stories: International Perspectives* (London: Routledge, 1999), p. 190.

36 See Brian Conway, 'Active Remembering, Selective Forgetting, and Collective Identity: The Case of Bloody Sunday', *Identity: An International Journal of Theory and Research* 3 (4), pp. 305–23.

37 Dawson, 'Trauma, Place and the Politics of Memory' p. 162. In this context Paul Connerton has written of the importance of the ritual of re-enactment for shaping communal memory; *How Societies Remember* (Cambridge: Cambridge University Press, 1989), p. 61. A reflection on this specifically in relation to Bloody Sunday can be found in Spillman and Conway, pp. 79–103.

38 Lewis A. Coser, (ed.), *Maurice Halbwachs' On Collective Memory* (Chicago: University of Chicago Press, 1992), p. 52.

39 Dawson, G. 'Trauma, Place and the Politics of Memory' p. 155.

40 Rafel Narvaez, 'Embodiment, Collective Memory and Time', *Body and Society* 12 (3): 2006, p. 66.

41 Malachy McDaid, quoted in Casciani, 'Creating a Virtual Bloody Sunday' (http://news.bbc.co.uk/1/hi/sci/tech/1791596.stm).

42 Clarke, C. Preliminary Hearing, Monday 20 July 1998 (www.bloody-sunday-inquiry.org; ph001), p. 10.

43 'It points to a future when all courtrooms will be equipped in this way to allow anyone, from those explaining what they saw in a minor traffic accident to the most complex law suits, to illustrate and record their views.' From Press Release, 'Northern Ireland e-Learning Developer Wins "Multimedia Oscar" at European Awards', Friday 23 February 2001 (http://www.rewardinglearning.com/development/new/press/2001/niclr.22.2.01.htm).

44 Sean Doran, 'The Lens and the Legal Practice: The Camera, the Court and the Reconstruction of Reality', *Source* 23: 2000, p. 23 (http://www.source.ie/issues/issues2140/issue23/is23artlenleg.html).

45 'Virtual reality may solve PC's murder' (http://news.bbc.co.uk/1/hi/england/2510575.stm).

46 Derrida, *Specters of Marx*, p. xix.

47 Ricoeur, p. 11.

CHAPTER 4: REPETITION AND RESTAGING

1 Gilles Deleuze, *Difference and Repetition* (London: Continuum, 2004), p. 3.

2 'The power of truth', *Guardian*, 10 June 2004 (http://film.guardian.co.uk/features/featurepages/0,,1235247,00.html).

3 Introduction (www.sunday-film.net).

4 Charles McDougall (dir.), *Sunday* (London: Channel 4, 2007), DVD.

5 Eamonn McCann, 'Far too much deference in this Derry', *Belfast Telegraph*, 21 January 2002, p. 15.

6 Paul Greengrass (dir.), *Bloody Sunday* (London: Feature Film Company, 2002), DVD.

7 Slavoj Žižek, 'On 9/11 New Yorkers faced the fire in the minds of men', *Guardian*, Monday 11 September 2006 (http://www.guardian.co.uk/comment/story/0,,1869353,00.html).

8 Paul de Man, *Blindness and Insight: Essays in the Rhetoric of Contemporary Criticism* (London: Routledge, 1983), p.xxi.

9 Martin McLoone, 'Bloody Sunday' [review], *Cineaste* xxvii: 2002, p. 43.

10 John Hill, *Cinema and Northern Ireland* (London: British Film Institute, 2006), p. 203.

11 Ibid., p. 204.

12 Mullan, p. xvii.

13 Hayden White, 'The Modernist Event' in Sobchack, V. (ed.) *The Persistence of History: Cinema, Television, and the Modernist Event* (London and New York: Routledge, 1996), p. 22.

14 Edward Said, *Beginnings: Intention and Method* (London: Granta, 1997), p. 50.

15 R. Penny, 'Bloody Sunday: Classically Unified Trauma' (available at http://www.film.ubc.ca/ubcinephile/cinephile/penney-bloodysunday.pdf).

16 Mary Ann Doane, 'The Voice in the Cinema: The Articulation of Body and Space', in P. Rosen (ed.), *Narrative, Apparatus, Ideology: A Film Theory Reader* (New York: Columbia University Press, 1986), p. 342.

17 McCann, E. 'Far too much deference in this Derry', p. 15.

18 Lyotard, p. 152.

19 Ibid., p. 16.

20 Giovanna Borradori, *Philosophy in a Time of Terror: Dialogues with Jürgen Habermas and Jacques Derrida* (Chicago: Chicago University Press, 2003), p. 34.

21 Laura U. Marks, *The Skin of the Film: Intercultural Cinema, Embodiment and the Senses* (Durham, NC: Duke University Press, 2000), p. 29.

22 Gilles Deleuze, *Cinema 2* (London: Athlone Press, 1989), pp. 245–55.

23 Cathy Caruth, *Unclaimed Experience: Trauma, Narrative, and History* (Baltimore and London: John Hopkins University Press, 1996), p. 4.

24 Jean-Jacques Lecercle, *Philosophy Through the Looking Glass* (La Salle: Open Court, 1985), p. 98.

25 Alain Badiou, *Being and Event* (London: Continuum, 2005).

26 Gilles Deleuze and Félix Guattari, *What Is Philosophy?* (London: Pluto Press, 1994), p. 110.

27 Lance Pettitt, 'Bloody Sunday: Dramatising Popular History in TV Film', in R. Gonzalez (ed.), *The Representation of Ireland/s: Images from Outside and from Within* (Barcelona: PPU, 2003), p. 56.

28 Lyotard, p. 13.

29 Luke Gibbons, 'Narratives of the Nation: Fact, Fiction and Irish Cinema', in L. Dodd (ed.), *Nationalism: Visions and Revisions* (Dublin: Film Institute of Ireland, 1999), p. 72.

30 Katie Kitamura, 'Recreating Chaos': Jeremy Deller's *The Battle of Orgreave*', paper given to the 'Extreme and Sentimental History' conference at University of Michigan at Ann Arbor, May 13–14 2005 (http://www.vanderbilt.edu/englishConference/papers.htm).

31 Carolyn Christov-Bakargiev and Caoimhín Mac Giolla Léith, *Willie Doherty: False Memory* (Dublin: Irish Museum of Modern Art, 2002), p. 17.

32 Quick, p. 157.

33 Christov-Bakargiev and Mac Giolla Léith, p. 12.
34 Marianne Elliott, *The Catholics of Ulster* (London: Penguin Books, 2001), p. 441.
35 Ricoeur, p. 9.
36 Deleuze, *Difference and Repetition*, pp. 1–2.

CHAPTER 5: IF WE DEAD AWAKENED

1 Czeslaw Milosz, 'Nobel Prize Lecture' (1980) (http://nobelprize.org/nobel_prizes/literature/laureates/1980/index.html).
2 Benjamin, p. 247.
3 Heaney released an abbreviated form of his ballad for publication some twenty-five years after the killings. It was first published in the *Derry Journal* on Friday 31 January 1997. Heaney's brief note to the poem makes clear that he intended it as a performance piece to be sung to the air of 'The Boys of Mullaghbawn' by Luke Kelly of The Dubliners.
4 Seamus Heaney, *Field Work* (London: Faber, 1979), p. 22.
5 For a fascinating reading of the song's Protestant redemptivism, see Barbara Bradby and Brian Torode, 'To Whom Do U2 Appeal?' *The Crane Bag* 8 (2): 1984, pp. 73–8.
6 Thomas Kinsella, 'Commentary' *Butcher's Dozen* (Dublin: Peppercanister Press, 2nd edition, 1992), p. 17.
7 Thomas Kinsella, *Fifteen Dead* (Dublin: Peppercanister Press, 1979), p. 54.
8 Ibid., p. 57.
9 Ibid., p. 58.
10 Northern Ireland Civil Rights Association, *Civil Rights* 1 (9): 13 May, 1972, p. 1.
11 Gerald Dawe, 'In the Violent Zone: *Thomas Kinsella's Nightwalker and Other Poems*', *Tracks* 7, 1987, p. 27.
12 Tom Paulin (ed.), *The Faber Book of Political Verse* (London: Faber, 1986), p. 19.
13 Kinsella, *Fifteen Dead*, p. xx.
14 Paulin, p. 19.
15 Seamus Deane, 'Foreword', in E. McCann, M. Shiels and B. Hannigan, *Bloody Sunday in Derry: What Really Happened* (Dingle: Brandon Books, 2000), p. 10.
16 Ibid., p. 12.
17 Seán Ó Tuama, 'Brian Merriman and his Court', *Irish University Review* 11 (2): 1981, p. 150.
18 Seán Ó Tuama (ed.) and Thomas Kinsella (trans.), *An Duanaire 1600–1900: Poems of the Dispossessed* (Dublin: Dolmen Press, 1981), p. 191.
19 Seamus Deane, *A Short History of Irish Literature* (London: Hutchinson, 1986), p. 23.
20 Ó Tuama, pp. 149, 158. It is striking to see how Seamus Heaney, in a review of Kinsella and Ó Tuama's *An Duanaire*, is himself more at ease in finding echoes between *Butcher's Dozen* and the 'classic' Jacobite *aisling* rather than Merriman's burlesque version: 'indeed the unrepentant note that he [Kinsella] appended to 'Butcher's Dozen' in his recent collection, *Fifteen Dead*, is continuous with the swell of political energy in . . . much of the work of Ó Bruadair, Ó Rathaille, Seán Clárach MacDomhnaill [that] has the same rage and certitude as Kinsella's own Bloody Sunday poem'. See Seamus Heaney, *The Government of the Tongue* (London: Faber, 1988), p. 32.
21 Seamus Heaney, 'Orpheus in Ireland: On Brian Merriman's *The Midnight Court*', *The Redress of Poetry* (London: Faber, 1995), p. 43.
22 Brian Merriman, *The Midnight Court* (trans. Ciaran Carson) (Oldcastle: Gallery Press, 2005), p. 33.
23 Heaney, 'Orpheus in Ireland', p. 47.
24 Ibid., p. 41.
25 Angela Hegarty, in conversation with the authors. This might have taken the form (perhaps with the Opsahl Commission in mind) of a People's Tribunal. The Opsahl Commission was a project organised by Initiative '92. Chaired by Norwegian Human Rights lawyer Torkel Opsahl, the commission heard submissions, during the months

of January and February 1993, from over 3,000 people at various locations across the North. The purpose of the Commission was to stimulate new ways of thinking about the conflict, and to encourage fresh approaches towards its eventual resolution.

26 Thomas Kinsella, *Butcher's Dozen* (Dublin: Peppercannister Press, 1972), p. 1.

27 James 3:14. *The Holy Bible*, Douay Version (London: Catholic Truth Society, 1956), p. 306.

28 Octave: a period of eight days that extends the celebration of a solemnity. The Christian year has two solemnities with octaves: Easter and Christmas.

29 The phrase is Heaney's adaptation of a line from Shakespeare's 'Sonnet 65'. See *Pre-occupations: Selected Prose 1968–1978* (London: Faber, 1980), p. 57.

30 Merriman, pp. 13–14.

31 Four men were, in fact, shot dead at the low rubble barricade: Michael Kelly, William Nash, John Young and Michael McDaid. See Peter Pringle and Philip Jacobson, *Those Are Real Bullets, Aren't They?* (London: Fourth Estate, 2001), pp. 159–82.

32 A certain hesitation is necessary here, because, as Derrida suggests in *Specters of Marx*, there can be no untroubled equation of ghost and the dead subject to which it is the apparent representation. 'We cannot identify it in all certainty', Derrida writes. 'It may always be a case of someone else still. Another can always lie, he can disguise himself as a ghost, another ghost may also be passing himself off for this one. It's always possible.' See Derrida, J. *Specters of Marx*, pp. 7–8. This hesitation is all the more necessary in relation to *Butcher's Dozen*, as none of the dead, nor their ghostly apparitions, are named.

33 Pringle and Jacobson, pp. 247–56.

34 Widgery, pp. 84–5.

35 Pringle and Jacobson, pp. 264–66.

36 Edna Longley, 'Spinning Through the Void', *Times Literary* Supplement, 19 December 1980, p. 1446.

37 The phrase seems to originate in Thomas Southerne's 1695 play *Oroonoko*, Act 1, Scene 1.

38 Jacques Derrida, *On Cosmopolitanism and Forgiveness* (London: Routledge, 2004), p. 32.

39 This is how Widgery deals with these deaths: 'These four men were all shot some-where near the south-west corner of the more northerly of the two courtyards of the flats at Glenfada Park. Their respective ages were 22, 35, 17 and 26. The two McKin-neys were not related. Three other men wounded in the same area were Quinn, O'Donnell and Friel. I deal with the cases of these four deceased together because I find the evidence too confused and too contradictory to make separate consideration possible.' See Widgery, pp. 80–1.

40 Eamonn McCann, Maureen Shiels and Bridie Hannigan, *Bloody Sunday in Derry: What Really Happened* (Dingle: Brandon Books, 2000).

41 Derval Tubridy, *Thomas Kinsella: The Peppercanister Poems* (Dublin: University College Dublin Press, 2001), p. 21.

42 But because this is a public poem, we, the readers, are also party to the drama unfolding in silence and as such we are in a realm similar to the dumbshows of six-teenth- and seventeenth-century English theatre; those shows-within-shows that constituted a commentary on, and an ironic supplement to, the main drama. *Butcher's Dozen* is a kind of spectral mummers play encouraging its audience to consider with a critical eye the larger drama that provoked the poem.

43 Stephen Greenblatt, *Shakespearean Negotiations: The Circulation of Social Energy in Renaissance England* (Oxford: Clarendon Press, 1988), p. 1.

CHAPTER 6: CASUALTIES OF LANGUAGE

1 Seamus Deane, 'Civilians and Barbarians', *Ireland's Field Day* (London: Hutchinson, 1985), p. 33.

2 Michel deMontaigne, 'On the Education of Children', *Essays* (trans. J. M. Cohen),

(Harmondsworth: Penguin, 1958), p. 70.

3 It is striking how many public demonstrations during the civil rights period culminated in a rally or a protest in Guildhall Square. There were other venues in the city centre for such gatherings (for example, Waterloo Place and The Diamond) but Guildhall Square had a particular resonance, symbolising, as it did, with the presence of the Guildhall on one side and the imposing city walls on the other, unionist misrule, in Derry in particular and in the province more widely. Being enclosed by buildings and the walls, it also had the best acoustics. Civil rights, unemployment and nationalist protests in Guildhall Square also took on an oppositional resonance in the very space in which, on an annual basis, the Apprentice Boys parade would remind the mainly Catholic inhabitants of the areas outside and under the walls of their permanent second-class status. There was considerable activity in the square at the exact time in which Friel's drama is set. On Friday 6 February, for example, crowds gathered around the Guildhall after a rally address by Rev. Ian Paisley. A protesting crowd 'ran towards Mr Paisley's supporters shouting "Burn the Union Jack"'. And on the following day NICRA held one of its nine province-wide demonstrations against the Public Order (Amendment) Act. The Act, which made it an offence to take part in an unlawful procession or sit-down demonstration with the intention of obstructing traffic, was passed at Stormont on Thursday 5 February. As this is only a few days before the play's action is set, it is reasonable to suppose that the protest march on which Lily, Michael and Skinner find themselves is one of these protests. See Richard Deutsch and Vivien Magowan, *Northern Ireland, 1968–1973: A Chronology of Events* (Belfast: Blackstaff Press, 1973), p. 60.

4 In addition to these already substantial troop formations, Friel adds the 8th Infantry Brigade.

5 Seamus Deane, 'Introduction', *Brian Friel: Plays 1* (London: Faber, 1984), p. 16.

6 Benjamin, p. 247.

7 Friel, B. *Brian Friel: Essays, Diaries, Interviews, 1964–1999* (London: Faber, 1999), p. 57.

8 Brian Friel, *Brian Friel: Essays, Diaries, Interviews, 1964–1999* (London: Faber, 1999), p. 57.

9 Ibid., p. 124. Compare this with Edward Daly's shocked response to Widgery: 'The Tribunal of Inquiry into the Bloody Sunday murders was over in double-quick time. Widgery submitted his findings to the Home Secretary and the House of Commons on 18 April. I received summaries by telephone from journalists early that afternoon and could not believe my ears. The doubters had been proved right. It was a whitewash. The guilty were found to be innocent. The innocent were found to be guilty. It was a complete travesty of justice . . . If the shootings were the first atrocity, the Widgery Report was the second atrocity associated with that fateful day.' See Daly, p. 211.

10 Friel moved from Omagh to Derry at the age of ten years. He lived in the Bogside, the area for which his father was a local government councillor, in which capacity Friel's father would have spent considerable time in the Guildhall.

11 Steven A. Nash and Robert Rosenblum (eds), *Picasso and the Wars Years, 1937–1945* (London: Thames & Hudson, 1998), p. 37.

12 Friel, p. 60.

13 On Wednesday 23 April 1969 the Unionist Parliamentary Party had voted by 28 to 22 to introduce universal adult suffrage in local government elections. The demand for 'one man, one vote' had been one of the most powerful slogans of the early civil rights movement.

14 Lionel Pilkington, *Theatre and the State in Twentieth-Century Ireland: Cultivating the People* (London: Routledge, 2001), p. 197.

15 Caruth.

16 *Oxford English Dictionary,* 1989.

17 Susan Cannon Harris, '"Watch Yourself": Performance, Sexual Difference and National Identity in the Plays of Frank McGuinness,' *Genders* 28 (1998)

(http://www.genders.org/g28/g28_watchyourself.txt Irish).

18 Ibid.

19 Caruth, p. 4.

20 Frank McGuinness, *Plays: One* (London: Faber, 1996), p. 7.

21 Saville, p. 1.

22 See website (www.bloody-sunday-inquiry.org.uk).

23 Bill Rolston, *Unfinished Business: State Killings and the Quest for Truth* (Belfast: Beyond the Pale Productions, 2000), p. 9.

24 Richard Norton-Taylor, *Bloody Sunday: Scenes from the Saville Inquiry* (London: Oberon Books, 2005), p. 18.

25 Ibid., p. 20.

26 Michael Billington, 'Bloody Sunday' [review], *Guardian*, 12 April 2005, p. 14.

Bibliography

Auslander, P. *Liveness: Performance in a Mediatized Culture* (London and New York: Routledge, 1999)

Badiou, A. *Being and Event* (London: Continuum, 2005)

Bakhtin, M. *The Dialogic Imagination*, (ed.) M. Holquist, (Austin: University of Texas Press, 1981)

Barthes, R. *Camera Lucida* (London: Vintage, 1993)

Bauman, Z. *Postmodern Ethics* (Oxford: Blackwell, 1993)

Benjamin, W. 'Theses on the Philosophy of History', in H. Zorn (ed.), *Illuminations* (London: Pimlico, 1999)

Bey, H. *T. A. Z. The Temporary Autonomous Zone, Ontological Anarchy, Poetic Terrorism* (Autonomedia Anti-copyright, 1985), (http://www.hermetic.com/bey/taz_cont.html)

Blair, T. *Parliamentary Debates* (*Hansard*) Sixth Series, Vol. 305, Col. 502 (29 January 1998)

Bloody Sunday Initiative. 'Programme of Events: Bloody Sunday 1972–1992' (1992)

Borradori, G. *Philosophy in a Time of Terror: Dialogues with Jürgen Habermas and Jacques Derrida* (Chicago: Chicago University Press, 2003)

Bradby, B., and B. Torode, 'To Whom Do U2 Appeal?' *The Crane Bag* 8 (2): 1984, pp. 73–8

Byrne, D. *Complexity Theory and the Social Sciences: An Introduction* (London: .Routledge, 1998)

Byrne, D. 'Complexity, Configurations and Cases', *Theory, Culture and Society* 22 (5): 2005, pp. 95–111

Canetti, E. *Crowds and Power* (London: Phoenix Press, 2000)

Caruth, C. *Unclaimed Experience: Trauma, Narrative, and History* (Baltimore and London: John Hopkins University Press, 1996)

Christov-Bakargiev, C., and C. Mac Giolla Léith, *Willie Doherty: False Memory* (Dublin: Irish Museum of Modern Art, 2002)

Connerton, P. *How Societies Remember* (Cambridge: Cambridge University Press, 1989)

Conway, B. 'Active Remembering, Selective Forgetting, and Collective Identity: The Case of Bloody Sunday', *Identity: An International Journal of Theory and Research* 3 (4), pp. 305–23

Crilly, A., and A. Hegarty, 'Remembering Bloody Sunday: The Role of Popular

Culture in Legal Process', paper presented to the 2004 Socio-Legal Studies Association Conference, Glasgow, 6–8 April 2004

Cunningham, W. 'Violent Conflict in Northern Ireland: Complex Life at the Edge of Chaos', paper presented to the 2001 National Conference on Peacemaking and Confict Resolution (NCPCR), George Mason University, Fairfax, Virginia, 7–10 June 2001 (http://cain.ulst.ac.uk/conflict/index.html)

Daly, E. *Mister, Are You a Priest?* (Dublin: Four Courts Press, 2000)

Dash, S. *Justice Denied: A Challenge to Lord Widgery's Report on 'Bloody Sunday'* (London: ILRM and NCCL, 1972)

Dawe, G. 'In the Violent Zone: *Thomas Kinsella's Nightwalker and Other Poems', Tracks* 7: 1987

Dawson, G. 'Trauma, Memory, Politics: The Irish Troubles', in K. Rogers (ed.), *Trauma and Life Stories: International Perspectives* (London: Routledge, 1999)

Dawson, G. 'Trauma, Place and the Politics of Memory: Bloody Sunday, Derry, 1972–2004', *History Workshop Journal* 59: 2005, pp. 151–78

de Man, P. *Blindness and Insight: Essays in the Rhetoric of Contemporary Criticism* (London and New York: Routledge, 1983)

Deane, S. 'Introduction', *Brian Friel: Plays One* (London: Faber, 1984)

—. 'Civilians and Barbarians', *Ireland's Field Day* (London: Hutchinson, 1985)

—. *A Short History of Irish Literature* (London: Hutchinson, 1986)

—. 'Foreword', in E. McCann, M. Shiels and B. Hannigan, *Bloody Sunday in Derry: What Really Happened* (Dingle: Brandon Books, 2000)

Delanda, M. *War in the Age of Intelligent Machines* (New York: Zone Books, 1991)

—. 'Nonorganic Life', in J. Crary and S. Kwinter (eds.), *Zone 6: Incorporations* (New York: Urzone, 1992)

—. *A Thousand Years of Nonlinear History* (New York: Swerve, 1997)

Deleuze, G. *Cinema 2* (London: The Athlone Press, 1989)

—. *Difference and Repetition* (London: Continuum, 2004)

Deleuze, G., and F. Guattari, *Kafka: Toward a Minor Literature* (Minneapolis: University of Minneapolis Press, 1986)

—. *A Thousand Plateaus* (London: The Athlone Press, 1988)

—. *What Is Philosophy?* (London: Pluto Press, 1994)

Deller, J. *The English Civil War – Part II: Personal Accounts of the 1984–85 Miners' Strikes* (London: Artangel, 2001)

Derrida, J. *Of Grammatology* (Baltimore and London: John Hopkins University Press, 1976)

—. *Specters of Marx: The State of the Debt, the Work of Mourning, and the New International* (New York and London: Routledge, 1994)

—. *On Cosmopolitanism and Forgiveness* (London: Routledge, 2004)

Deutsch, R., and V. Magowan, *Northern Ireland, 1968–1973: A Chronology of Events* (Belfast: Blackstaff Press, 1973)

Doane, M. A. 'The Voice in the Cinema: The Articulation of Body and Space', in P. Rosen (ed.), *Narrative, Apparatus, Ideology: A Film Theory Reader* (New York: Columbia University Press, 1986)

Doherty, P. *Paddy Bogside* (Cork: Mercier Press, 2001)

Doran, S. 'The Lens and the Legal Practice: The Camera, the Court and the

Reconstruction of Reality', *Source* 23: 2000 (http://www.source.ie/issues/ issues2140/issue23/is23artlenleg.html)

Dubois, P. *L'Acte Photographique* (Paris and Brussels: Nathan/Labor, 1983)

Duggan, D. *Scenes from an Inquiry* (Derry: Sole Purpose Productions, 1997)

Dunn, S. 'Bloody Sunday and Its Commemoration Parades', in T. G. Fraser (ed.), *Irish Parading Tradition: Following the Drum* (Gordonsville, VA: Palgrave Macmillan, 2000)

Elliott, M. *The Catholics of Ulster* (London: Penguin Books, 2001)

Friel, B. *Brian Friel: Essays, Diaries, Interviews, 1964–1999* (London: Faber, 1999)

Gibbons, L. 'Narratives of the Nation: Fact, Fiction and Irish Cinema', in L. Dodd (ed.), *Nationalism: Visions and Revisions* (Dublin: Film Institute of Ireland, 1999)

Goodrich, P. *Languages of Law: From Logics of Memory to Nomadic Masks* (London: Weidenfeld & Nicolson, 1990)

Greenblatt, S. *Shakespearean Negotiations: The Circulation of Social Energy in Renaissance England* (Oxford: Clarendon Press, 1988)

Greengrass, P. (dir.) *Bloody Sunday* (London: Feature Film Company, 2002), DVD

Gripsrud, J. *Understanding Media Culture* (London: Arnold, 2002)

Halbwachs, M., *On Collective Memory* (translated and edited by Coser, L.A.) (Chicago: University of Chicago Press, 1992)

Hardt, M., and A. Negri, *Multitude* (London: Penguin, 2004)

Hardt, M., and A. Negri, *Empire* (Cambridge, MA: Harvard University Press, 2000)

Harris, S. C., '"Watch Yourself": Performance, Sexual Difference and National Identity in the Plays of Frank McGuinness', *Genders* 28: 1998 (http://www.genders.org/g28/g28_watchyourself.txt Irish)

Hayes, P., and J. Campbell, *Bloody Sunday: Trauma, Pain and Politics* (London: Pluto Press, 2005)

Hegarty, A. 'Truth, Law and Official Denial: The Case of Bloody Sunday', *Criminal Law Forum* 15 (1/2): 2004, pp. 199–246

Heaney, S. *Field Work* (London: Faber, 1979)

—. *Preoccupations: Selected Prose 1968–1978* (London: Faber, 1980)

—. *The Government of the Tongue* (London: Faber, 1988)

—. 'Orpheus in Ireland: On Brian Merriman's *The Midnight Court*', *The Redress of Poetry* (London: Faber, 1995)

Hegarty, A. 'Truth, Law and Official Denial: The Case of Bloody Sunday', *Criminal Law Forum* 15 (1/2): 2004, p. 199

Hill, J. *Cinema and Northern Ireland* (London: British Film Institute, 2006)

Ignatieff, M. 'Articles of Faith', *Index on Censorship* 25 (5): 1996, p. 113

Jarman, N. *Material Conflicts: Parades and Visual Displays in Northern Ireland* (Oxford: Berg, 1997)

Jung, H. W. 'Bakhtin's Dialogical Body Politics', in M. M. Bell and M. Gardiner (eds.), *Bakhtin and the Human Sciences* (London: Sage, 1998)

Kearney, R., and M. Dooley (eds.), *Questioning Ethics: Contemporary Debates in Philosophy* (London and New York: Routledge, 1998)

Kelly, W. Email correspondence with the authors (30 November 2005)

Kerr, A. (ed.) *No Go: A Photographic Record of Free Derry* (L'Derry: Guildhall Press, 1997)

Kinsella, T. *Butcher's Dozen* (Dublin: Peppercanister Press, 1972)

Kinsella, T. *Fifteen Dead* (Dublin: Peppercanister Press, 1979)

Kinsella, T. 'Commentary', *Butcher's Dozen* (Dublin: Peppercanister Press, 2nd edition, 1992)

Kitamura, K. 'Recreating Chaos: Jeremy Deller's *The Battle of Orgreave*', paper given to the 'Extreme and Sentimental History' conference at University of Michigan at Ann Arbor, 13–14 May 2005 (http://www.vanderbilt. edu/englishConference/papers.htm)

Lecercle, J-J. *Philosophy Through the Looking Glass* (La Salle: Open Court, 1985)

Levinas, E. 'An Interview', in R. Bernasconi and D. Wood (eds.), *The Provocation of Levinas: Rethinking the Other* (London: Routledge, 1988)

Loftus, E. 'Our changeable memories: Legal and practical implications', *Nature Reviews Neuroscience* 4: March 2003

Longley, E. 'Spinning Through the Void', *Times Literary Supplement*, 19 December 1980, p. 1446

Lyotard, J-F. *The Différend: Phrases in Dispute* (Minneapolis: University of Minnesota Press, 1988)

Marks, L. U. *The Skin of the Film: Intercultural Cinema, Embodiment and the Senses* (Durham, NC: Duke University Press, 2000)

Massumi, B. *A User's Guide to Capitalism and Schizophrenia: Deviations from Deleuze and Guattari* (Cambridge, MA, and London: MIT Press, 1992)

McCann, E. 'Far too much deference in this Derry', *Belfast Telegraph*, 21 January 2002

McCann, E. (ed.) *The Bloody Sunday Inquiry: The Families Speak Out* (London: Pluto Press, 2005)

McCann, E., M. Shiels and B. Hannigan, *Bloody Sunday in Derry: What Really Happened* (Dingle: Brandon Books, 2000)

McDougall, C. (dir.) *Sunday* (London: Channel 4, 2007), DVD

McGuinness, F. *Carthaginians* and *Baglady* (London: Faber, 1988)

McGuinness, F. *Plays: One* (London: Faber, 1996)

McGuinness, M., and G. Downey, *Creggan: More Than a History* (L'Derry: Guildhall Press, 2000)

McLoone, M. 'Bloody Sunday' [review], *Cineaste* xxvii: 2002, p. 4

Megill, A. 'History, Memory, Identity', *History of the Human Sciences* 11 (3): 1998, pp. 37–62

Merriman, B. *The Midnight Court* (trans. Ciaran Carson) (Oldcastle: Gallery Press, 2005)

Milosz, C. 'Nobel Prize Lecture', 1980 (http://nobelprize.org/nobel_prizes/ literature/laureates/1980/index.html)

Montaigne, M. de 'On the Education of Children', *Essays* (trans. J. M. Cohen) (Harmondsworth: Penguin, 1958)

Morris, P. *The Bakhtin Reader* (London and New York: Arnold, 1994)

Mullan, D. *Eyewitness Bloody Sunday: The Truth* (London: Merlin, 3rd edition, 2002)

Narvaez, R. 'Embodiment, Collective Memory and Time', *Body and Society* 12 (3): 2006, pp. 51–73

Nora, P. 'Between Memory and History: *Les Lieux de Mémoire*', *Representations* 26: Spring 1989, pp. 7–24

Nash, S. A., and R. Rosenblum (eds.), *Picasso and the War Years, 1937–1945* (London: Thames & Hudson, 1998)

Norton-Taylor, R. *Bloody Sunday: Scenes from the Saville Inquiry* (London: Oberon Books, 2005)

Ó Dochartaigh, N. *From Civil Rights to Armalites: Derry and the Birth of the Irish Troubles* (Cork: Cork University Press, 1997)

Ó Tuama, S. 'Brian Merriman and His Court', *Irish University Review* 11 (2): 1981, p. 150

Ó Tuama, S. (ed.) and T. Kinsella (trans.) *An Duanaire 1600–1900: Poems of the Dispossessed* (Dublin: Dolmen Press, 1981)

O'Brien, J. *A Matter of Minutes: The Enduring Legacy of Bloody Sunday* (Dublin: Wolfhound Press, 2002)

Patton, P. *Deleuze and the Political* (Routledge, London, 2000)

Paulin, T. (ed.) *The Faber Book of Political Verse* (London: Faber, 1986)

Penny, R. 'Bloody Sunday: Classically Unified Trauma' (http://www.film.ubc.ca/ubcinephile/cinephile/penney-bloodysunday.pdf)

Pettitt, L. 'Bloody Sunday: Dramatising Popular History in TV Film', in R. Gonzalez (ed.), *The Representation of Ireland/s: Images from Outside and from Within* (Barcelona: PPU, 2003)

Pilkington, L. *Theatre and the State in Twentieth-Century Ireland: Cultivating the People* (London: Routledge, 2001)

Pringle, P., and P. Jacobson, *Those Are Real Bullets, Aren't They?* (London: Fourth Estate, 2001)

Purdie, B. *Politics in the Streets: The Origins of the Civil Rights Movement in Northern Ireland* (Belfast: Blackstaff Press, 1990)

Quick, A. 'The Space Between: Photography and the Time of Forgetting in the Work of Willie Doherty', in A. Kuhn and K.E. McAllister (eds.), *Locating Memory: Photographic Acts* (New York and Oxford: Berghahn Books, 2006)

Ricoeur, P. 'Memory and Forgetting', in R. Kearney and M. Dooley (eds.), *Questioning Ethics: Contemporary Debates in Continental Philosophy* (London: Routledge, 1998)

Rolston, B. *Unfinished Business: State Killings and the Quest for Truth* (Belfast: Beyond the Pale Productions, 2000), p. 9.

Rudé, G. *The Face of the Crowd: Studies in Revolution, Ideology and Popular Protest* (New York and London: Harvester Wheatsheaf, 1988)

Said, E. *Beginnings: Intention and Method* (London: Granta, 1997)

Santino, J. *Signs of War and Peace: Social Conflict and the Uses of Symbols in Public in Northern Ireland* (New York: Palgrave Macmillan, 2001)

Saville, M. 'Letter to Mr Michael McKinney and Mr John Kelly' (24 October 2006)

Serres, M. *Genesis* (Ann Arbor: University of Michigan Press, 1995)

Sontag, S. *On Photography* (London: Penguin, 1977)

Spilllman, L., and B. Conway 'Texts, Bodies, and the Memory of Bloody Sunday', *Symbolic Interaction* 30 (1): 2007, pp. 79–103

Stallybrass, P., and A. White, *The Politics and Poetics of Transgression* (Ithaca: Cornell University Press, 1986)

Sutton, M. *An Index of Deaths from the Conflict in Northern Ireland 1969–1993* (Belfast: Beyond the Pale Publications, 2006) (updated version available at www.cain.ulst.ac.uk)

Tagg, J. *The Burden of Representation: Essays on Photographies and Histories* (Basingstoke: Macmillan, 1988)

Taylor, P. 'Turning a blind eye to murder', *Guardian*, Friday 18 April 2003

Terdiman, R. *Present Past: Modernity and the Memory Crisis* (Ithaca and London: Cornell University Press, 1993)

Tereshchuk, D. 'Through a Glass Darkly: Memories of Bloody Sunday' (2006) (www.tereshchuk.com/go/on/archived/art/3845)

Thoburn, N. *Deleuze, Marx and Politics* (London: Routledge, 2003)

Tubridy, D. *Thomas Kinsella: The Peppercanister Poems* (Dublin: University College Dublin Press, 2001)

Urry, J. *Global Complexity* (Cambridge: Polity Press, 2003)

—. 'The Complexity Turn' *Theory, Culture and Society* 22 (5): 2005, pp. 1–14

Valverde, M. 'Derrida's Justice and Foucault's Freedom: Ethics, History, and Social Movements', *Law and Social Inquiry* 24 (3): 1999, pp. 655–76

Virilio, P. *Speed and Politics* (New York: Semiotext(e), 1986)

Walsh, D. *Bloody Sunday and the Rule of Law in Northern Ireland* (Houndmills: Macmillan, 2000)

Weissberg, L., and D. Ben-Amos (eds.), *Cultural Memory and the Construction of Identity* (Detroit: Wayne State University, 1999)

White, G. D. '"Quite a Profound Day": The Public Performance of Memory by Military Witnesses at the Bloody Sunday Tribunal', *Theatre Research International* 31 (2): 2006, pp. 174–87

White, H. 'The Modernist Event', in V. Sobchack (ed.), *The Persistence of History: Cinema, Television, and the Modernist Event* (London and New York: Routledge, 1996)

Widgery, J. *Bloody Sunday, 1972* (London: HMSO, 2001). Originally published as the *Report of the Tribunal appointed to inquire into the events on Sunday, 30th January 1972, which led to the loss of life in connection with the procession in Londonderry on that day by The Rt. Hon. Lord Widgery, OBE, TD* (HMSO, 1972)

www.museumoffreederry.org/history-bloody-reaction.html

Ziff, T. (ed.) *Hidden Truths: Bloody Sunday 1972* (Santa Monica: Smart Art Press, 1998)

Žižek, S. 'On 9/11 New Yorkers faced the fire in the minds of men', *Guardian*, 11 September 2006

Index